AMERICAN POLITICAL, ECONOMIC, AND SECURITY ISSUES

SUPPLY CHAIN SECURITY

CARGO CONTAINER AND FEDERAL INFORMATION TECHNOLOGY PROCUREMENT RISKS

American Political, Economic, and Security Issues

Additional books in this series can be found on Nova's website under the Series tab.

Additional E-books in this series can be found on Nova's website under the E-book tab.

AMERICAN POLITICAL, ECONOMIC, AND SECURITY ISSUES

SUPPLY CHAIN SECURITY

CARGO CONTAINER AND FEDERAL INFORMATION TECHNOLOGY PROCUREMENT RISKS

MARTEN LAURITS
EDITOR

New York

For permission to use material from this book please contact us:
Telephone 631-231-7269; Fax 631-231-8175
Web Site: http://www.novapublishers.com

Library of Congress Cataloging-in-Publication Data

ISBN: 978-1-62808-230-2

Published by Nova Science Publishers, Inc. † New York

CONTENTS

PREFACE

The U.S. economy is dependent on the expeditious flow of millions of tons of cargo each day. Cargo containers are an important instrument of global trade but also can present security concerns. U.S. Customs and Border Protection (CBP), within the Department of Homeland Security (DHS), is responsible for administering container security programs, and its strategy for securing maritime cargo containers includes analyzing information to identify shipments that may contain terrorist weapons or other contraband. Because CBP has insufficient resources to examine every container, targeters use Automated Targeting Systems (ATS) to profile which container shipments should be examined. This book addresses how ATS supports CBP's targeting of maritime cargo container shipments for national security purposes; and the extent to which CBP assesses the effectiveness of ATS's national security targeting rules.

Chapter 1 – Report of United States Government Accountability Office, on Supply Chain Security: CBP Needs to Conduct Regular Assessments of Its Cargo Targeting System, dated October 2012.

Chapter 2 – Report of United States Government Accountability Office, on IT Supply Chain: National Security-Related Agencies Need to Better Address Risks, dated March 2012.

In: Supply Chain Security
Editor: Marten Laurits

ISBN: 978-1-62808-230-2

Chapter 1

SUPPLY CHAIN SECURITY: CBP NEEDS TO CONDUCT REGULAR ASSESSMENTS OF ITS CARGO TARGETING SYSTEM*

United States Government Accountability Office

WHY GAO DID THIS STUDY

The U.S. economy is dependent on the expeditious flow of millions of tons of cargo each day. Cargo containers are an important instrument of global trade but also can present security concerns. CBP is responsible for administering container security programs, and its strategy for securing maritime cargo containers includes analyzing information to identify shipments that may contain terrorist weapons or other contraband. Because CBP has insufficient resources to examine every container, targeters use ATS to target which container shipments should be examined. GAO was asked to assess CBP's targeting efforts. This report addresses (1) how ATS supports CBP's targeting of maritime cargo container shipments for national security purposes and (2) the extent to which CBP assesses the effectiveness of ATS's national security targeting rules. GAO analyzed fiscal year 2011 CBP data on shipments and containers arriving at U.S. ports and containers scanned at these ports. GAO also visited six CBP units selected on the basis of the percentage

* This is an edited, reformatted and augmented version of United States Government Accountability Office, Publication No. GAO-13-9, dated October 2012.

of maritime shipments that were scored as high risk or medium risk for national security purposes at these locations in fiscal year 2011, among other factors. GAO also analyzed documents, such as CBP's ATS performance measures.

WHAT GAO RECOMMENDS

GAO recommends that CBP (1) ensure that future updates to the weight set are based on assessments of its performance and (2) establish targets for performance measures and use those measures to regularly assess effectiveness of the weight set. DHS concurred with these recommendations.

WHAT GAO FOUND

U.S. Customs and Border Protection (CBP), within the Department of Homeland Security (DHS), employs a risk-based approach that uses the Automated Targeting System (ATS) and other tools to identify (target) maritime cargo shipments for further examination. ATS is a web-based enforcement and decision support system that includes a set of rules to assess the risk level for each arriving cargo shipment. This set of rules is referred to as the maritime national security weight set (weight set) because each rule in the set has a specific weighted value assigned to it. CBP classifies the risk scores from the weight set as low, medium, or high risk. CBP policy states that a shipment's risk score is to determine, in part, actions taken by CBP officers (targeters) at the ports. Specifically, targeters are generally required to review shipment data for all medium-risk and high-risk shipments and hold high-risk shipments for examination. The risk score, however, is not the sole factor that determines whether a targeter reviews the data for a shipment or whether CBP examines a shipment. In particular, targeters at each of the six ports GAO visited explained that they use the ATS risk score as a starting point for the targeting process but that their decisions regarding which shipments to examine are ultimately based on additional research. Targeters at the six ports GAO visited said they also use tools outside of ATS, such as web searches, to research shipments.

CBP efforts to assess the weight set's effectiveness in identifying the risk of shipments have been limited. CBP has performance measures—represented by the percentage of shipments targeted as high risk that contain a threat and the percentage of shipments targeted as high risk that do not contain a threat—that enable CBP to determine the accuracy of the weight set, given a particular workload or examination rate. However, CBP did not assess the weight set to verify its effectiveness when implementing an updated version in early 2011. Prior to implementing the updated version of the weight set, CBP assessed the potential impact of the update on CBP's workload but did not conduct an assessment to determine whether the updated version of the weight set would be more effective in identifying high-risk shipments than the previous version or other alternatives. Assessing the potential effectiveness of alternative versions of the weight set prior to selecting one for implementation could help CBP make more informed decisions about future updates. Doing so could also provide CBP reasonable assurance that the version it selects is the most effective of the alternatives and is more effective than the previous version it replaces. Furthermore, since implementing the updated version of the weight set in early 2011, CBP has not regularly assessed the weight set to monitor its performance and to help determine when changes are needed. For example, CBP conducted the first assessment of the current version of the weight set, using the performance measures, in the summer of 2012—18 months after the weight set's implementation in early 2011. Regular assessments of the weight set's effectiveness could help CBP determine when updates are needed in a timelier manner and ensure that targeters have the best information available to make targeting decisions. Moreover, CBP has not established targets for the performance measures so that it is not clear whether a particular change in the weight set's performance is significant enough to suggest that changes are needed to improve the effectiveness of the weight set.

ABBREVIATIONS

A&T	Analysis and Targeting Division
ATS	Automated Targeting System
ATU	Advance Targeting Unit
CBP	U.S. Customs and Border Protection
CERTS	Cargo Enforcement Reporting and Tracking System
DHS	Department of Homeland Security
FMFIA	Federal Managers' Financial Integrity Act
FPR	false positive rate
NII	nonintrusive inspection

NTC-C	National Targeting Center–Cargo
OIG	Office of Inspector General
OMB	Office of Management and Budget
TPR	true positive rate
WMD	weapons of mass destruction

October 25, 2012

The Honorable Susan M. Collins
Ranking Member
Committee on Homeland Security
and Governmental Affairs United States Senate

The Honorable Cliff Stearns
Chairman

The Honorable Diana DeGette
Ranking Member
Subcommittee on Oversight and Investigations
Committee on Energy and Commerce
House of Representatives

The economic well-being of the United States is dependent on the expeditious flow of millions of tons of cargo each day. According to the U.S. Department of Transportation, the majority of U.S. imports arrive by ocean vessel, and much of that is transported in cargo containers.[1] In fiscal year 2011, for example, about 13.4 million cargo containers arrived at U.S. seaports. Cargo containers are an important segment of the global supply chain—the flow of goods from manufacturers to retailers— and can present significant security concerns. Within the federal government, U.S. Customs and Border Protection (CBP), part of the Department of Homeland Security (DHS), is responsible for administering container security and reducing the vulnerabilities associated with the supply chain. Balancing security concerns with the need to facilitate the free flow of commerce, part of CBP's mission, remains an ongoing challenge for the public and private sectors alike.[2] CBP officials believe that the likelihood of terrorists smuggling weapons of mass destruction (WMD) into the United States in cargo containers is relatively low; however, the consequences of such an event could be catastrophic.

Although there have been no known incidents of cargo containers being used to transport WMD, ensuring the security of cargo containers remains an important role for CBP given that criminals have exploited containers for other illegal purposes, such as smuggling weapons, people, and illicit substances.

Since September 11, 2001, Congress has passed various laws to address concerns about the security of cargo containers in the global supply chain. The enactment of the Maritime Transportation Security Act of 2002[3] called for the establishment of a program to evaluate and certify secure systems of international intermodal transportation, including standards and procedures for screening and evaluating cargo containers prior to loading onto vessels and for securing and monitoring cargo while in transit.[4] In 2006, the Security and Accountability For Every Port Act was enacted,[5] which required, among other things, that pilot projects be established at three ports to test the feasibility of scanning 100 percent of U.S.-bound cargo containers at foreign ports.[6] Subsequently, the Implementing Recommendations of the 9/11 Commission Act of 2007 (9/11 Act)[7] required, among other things, that by July 2012, 100 percent of U.S.-bound cargo containers be scanned at foreign ports with both radiation detection and nonintrusive inspection (NII) equipment before being placed on U.S.-bound vessels.[8] In May 2012, the Secretary of Homeland Security authorized a 2-year extension—until July 2014—of the deadline for implementing the requirement that containers not enter the United States unless they were scanned at foreign ports prior to being loaded on vessels.[9]

We reported in October 2009 that CBP faced numerous challenges in implementing 100 percent scanning at pilot ports, and on the basis of work we have completed since then we know that CBP has not yet achieved 100 percent scanning.[10] In October 2009, we recommended, among other things, that CBP conduct a feasibility analysis of implementing the 100 percent scanning requirement and provide the results to Congress along with any suggestions of cost-effective alternatives to implementing the 100 percent scanning requirement, as appropriate. DHS stated that CBP concurred with these recommendations, but CBP has not yet taken action to address them. In its report to Congress in May 2012 on the planned deadline extension, DHS stated that it recognizes the need to proceed with container security programs in a manner that maximizes the security of maritime cargo and facilitates its movement and reported that it plans to continue working with other federal agencies and international partners to develop technology and enhance risk management processes, in addition to continuing existing programs that enhance cargo security.[11] However, given that the feasibility of 100 percent scanning remains in doubt and DHS and CBP have not identified alternatives that could achieve the same goals as 100 percent scanning, uncertainty persists regarding the scope of DHS's and CBP's existing container security programs and how these programs will collectively affect the movement of goods between trading partners.

CBP's strategy for securing the maritime supply chain consists of programs that intersect with key points in the supply chain. These programs include, among other things, analyzing information to identify shipments that may be at high risk of transporting WMD or other contraband; working with foreign governments to examine U.S.-bound, high-risk shipments at foreign ports; and examining U.S.-bound, high-risk shipments that were not examined overseas upon their arrival at a domestic port.[12] To aid in this process, CBP uses the Automated Targeting System (ATS), which is an intranet-based enforcement and decision support system that compares traveler, cargo, and conveyance information against intelligence and other enforcement data. Among other things, ATS uses a set of rules that assess different factors in data provided by supply chain parties, such as importers, to determine the risk level for a shipment. CBP officers (targeters) use information in ATS to identify (target) which shipments should be held for an examination, which may include an NII scan or a physical inspection.[13] Because CBP does not scan 100 percent of U.S.-bound cargo containers, the effectiveness of CBP's security strategy depends on CBP's ability to use ATS, among other tools, to effectively target shipments in the supply chain that pose the greatest security risks.

In response to your request, we analyzed certain aspects of CBP's maritime national security targeting efforts. Specifically, this report addresses the following objectives:

- How does ATS support CBP's process for targeting maritime cargo container shipments for national security purposes?
- To what extent does CBP assess the effectiveness of the national security targeting rules in ATS?

To address the first objective, we obtained data from CBP for each of the 115 U.S. seaports for fiscal year 2011 on the number of (1) shipments it placed in each of three categories—high risk, medium risk, and low risk— arriving at each of the ports;[14] (2) container arrivals at these ports; and (3) containers scanned at these ports using NII equipment. We selected and visited six CBP units responsible for targeting at domestic ports. Specifically, these ports were selected from among the largest ports in the United States using the following criteria:[15] (1) the percentage of maritime shipments that were scored as high risk or medium risk for national security purposes, (2) the percentage of cargo containers that were examined using NII equipment, and (3) whether a CBP official from the port participated in the most recent CBP conference to discuss changes to ATS cargo targeting rules.[16] The six targeting units we visited were responsible for targeting efforts at 15 ports that collectively received about 60 percent of the maritime shipments that arrived in the United States in fiscal year 2011. As part of these site visits, we observed port operations, including the scanning of containers. At each location, we also interviewed CBP targeters, including those who participated in the most recent CBP conference to discuss changes to cargo targeting rules, and observed their use of ATS and other tools to conduct cargo targeting activities. The results from our visits to these six targeting units cannot be generalized to ports nationwide; however, visits to these locations allowed us to directly observe the targeting process and provided insights into how ATS assigns risk scores to maritime shipments and how CBP integrates the scores into its targeting process. We synthesized the information from these site visits to describe the targeting process and also analyzed CBP policies and guidance, such as CBP's National Maritime Targeting Policy and course materials from CBP's Sea Cargo Targeting Training. We also visited CBP's National Targeting Center–Cargo (NTC-C) to interview targeters responsible for conducting national-level targeting and to observe their targeting activities.[17]

To address the second objective, we analyzed CBP's performance measures related to CBP's national security targeting rules in ATS that are used to assess potential risks in maritime cargo container shipments. These performance measures include the true positive rate and false positive rate, as discussed later in this report. In particular, we reviewed a consulting firm's evaluation of ATS from 2006 and CBP's project plan for implementing the most recent update to the targeting rules, including CBP's plans for monitoring ATS through the use of performance measures and an established methodology. We also reviewed our past work on ATS and its effectiveness, as well as an audit report from the DHS Office of Inspector General.[18] The Office of Inspector General's assessment of CBP's modifications to the ATS national security targeting rules was based on a series of interviews with agency officials and a review of relevant documentation and was sufficient to address the issue of documentation of changes to the ATS rules that we present in this report. We analyzed documentation of CBP's most recent update to the national security targeting rules, which CBP implemented in early 2011, and the extent to which this documentation addressed effectiveness. Specifically, we evaluated CBP's impact assessments, which provide information on the number of shipments the updated rules would assess as high risk, thereby affecting CBP's examination workload. In addition, we evaluated the extent to which CBP used its methodology to assess the current national security targeting rules and analyzed the results of CBP's assessments. To assess the reliability of the results of CBP's assessments, we reviewed documentation on the methodology created for CBP by a consulting firm in 2006.

We interviewed knowledgeable CBP officials about any adjustments to this methodology since the contract expired and CBP analysts began conducting the performance assessments. On the basis of this information we determined that the results of the assessments are sufficiently reliable for the purposes of our report. To determine the extent to which CBP conducts such assessments on a regular basis, we analyzed documentation of recent assessments of the national security targeting rules conducted in spring 2011 and summer 2012. We compared this information with key elements for a risk management approach and *Standards for Internal Control in the Federal Government.*[19]

We also reviewed our prior work on risk management practices and compared our analysis of CBP's actions and assessments with those practices. Finally, we interviewed officials at CBP headquarters who are responsible for maintaining and updating ATS to obtain information on past efforts to assess and update the national security targeting rules.

DHS deemed some of the information in a draft version of this report as sensitive, and therefore, this report omits sensitive details regarding specific information available in ATS, examples of how targeters may use that information, and specific dates associated with changes to CBP's targeting criteria. These omissions did not affect the presentation of the key information and findings that support our conclusions and recommendations.

We conducted our work from October 2011 through October 2012 in accordance with generally accepted government auditing standards. Those standards require that we plan and perform the audit to obtain sufficient, appropriate evidence to provide a reasonable basis for our findings and conclusions based on our audit objectives. We believe that the evidence obtained provides a reasonable basis for our findings and conclusions based on our audit objectives.

BACKGROUND

CBP's Maritime Cargo Container Security Strategy

CBP's security strategy for maritime cargo uses a risk-based approach to focus limited resources on targeting and examining cargo shipments that pose a potential risk while allowing other cargo shipments to proceed without unduly disrupting commerce into or out of the United States.

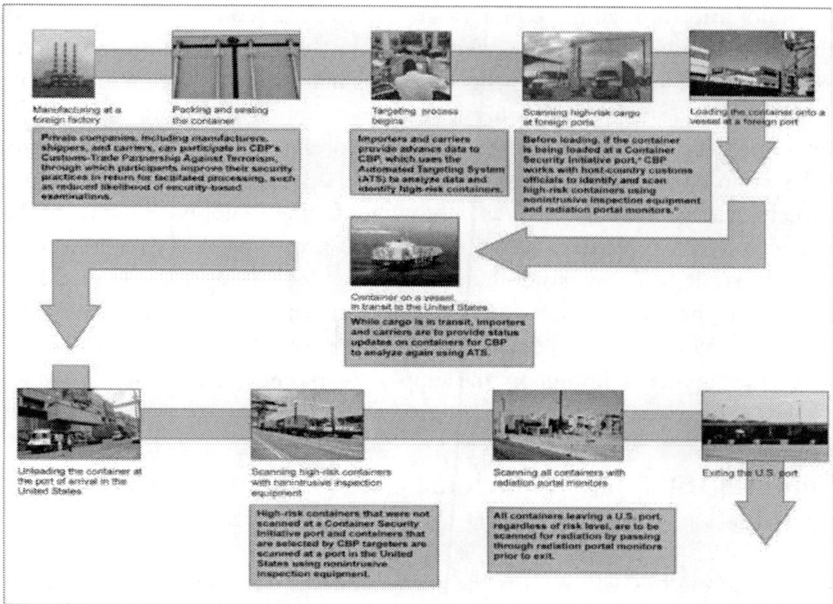

Source: GAO (analysis and photos) and CBP and DHS Science and Technology Directorate (photos).

[a]The Container Security Initiative places CBP staff at participating foreign ports to work with host country customs officials to target and examine high-risk cargo containers for WMD before they are shipped to the United States. CBP officials identify the containers that may pose a risk for terrorism and request that their foreign counterparts examine the contents of the containers.

[b]Host government officials at foreign ports that do not participate in the Container Security Initiative may also scan containers using radiation portal monitors as part of their operations.

Figure 1. Key Steps for Targeting High-Risk Shipments throughout the Maritime Supply Chain Process.

The strategy is based, in part, on obtaining advance cargo information. In particular, through what is referred to as the 24-hour rule, CBP generally requires vessel carriers to electronically transmit cargo manifests to CBP 24 hours before cargo is loaded onto U.S.-bound vessels at foreign ports.[20] Through the Importer Security Filing and Additional Carrier Requirements (known as the 10+2 rule), CBP requires importers and vessel carriers to provide data elements for improved identification of containerized cargo shipments that may pose a risk for terrorism.[21] Importers are responsible for supplying CBP with 10 shipping data elements—such as country of origin—24 hours prior to loading, while vessel carriers are required to provide 2 data elements—container status messages and stow plans[22]—that are not required by the 24-hour rule. Other aspects of CBP's maritime cargo container security strategy include using technology, such as radiation detection equipment, to detect potential threats and partnering with foreign governments and the trade industry to examine containers prior to their arrival in the United States and implement security measures throughout the supply chain process, respectively. A brief description of the core programs that constitute CBP's security strategy for cargo containers is provided in appendix I. Throughout the supply chain process, and underlying many of the programs within CBP's security strategy for cargo containers, CBP assesses the national security risks posed by shipments throughout the supply chain process, as shown in figure 1.

Role of ATS in CBP's Maritime Cargo Container Security Strategy

According to CBP, ATS is the cornerstone of CBP's targeting efforts that underlie the other programs that constitute CBP's security strategy for maritime cargo containers. CBP targeters review shipment records in ATS prior to the cargo being loaded onto U.S.-bound vessels, during shipment transit, and upon arrival at domestic ports to identify potential threats and determine if additional action, such as an examination, is required. When shipment data are updated with additional or amended information, CBP targeters using ATS might identify new risks or mitigate previously identified risks. These targeting efforts, and their reliance on ATS, are key to the operations of CBP's other security programs. For example, through ATS, CBP determines which shipments may be scanned overseas as part of the Container Security Initiative in an effort to prevent potentially dangerous cargo from being loaded onto U.S.- bound vessels. Additionally, through ATS, CBP is able to reduce the likelihood of examinations for members of the Customs-Trade Partnership Against Terrorism. The Customs-Trade Partnership Against Terrorism is a program through which CBP provides facilitated processing, such as reduced likelihood of security-based examinations, for members that implement the program's minimum security criteria or guidelines and best practices.

The overall effectiveness of CBP's strategy for securing maritime cargo containers depends largely on the effectiveness of ATS. We have previously reported on CBP's efforts to assess the effectiveness of ATS and have made recommendations to help CBP achieve the objectives of its overall maritime cargo targeting strategy. In response to these recommendations, CBP has made improvements to ATS and its targeting process, but in some cases CBP's implementation efforts have been slow, leaving CBP without the benefits of these improvements for several years. For more information about our prior work and recommendations regarding ATS, see appendix II.

ATS and National Security Targeting Rules

CBP targeters use ATS in the targeting process to help them determine whether to take further security actions, such as holding the shipment for examination, for cargo shipments they are reviewing. ATS consolidates data from various sources to create a single, comprehensive record for each U.S.-bound shipment. For example, carriers and importers provide data in compliance with the 24-hour rule and the 10+2 rule through other CBP systems, and these systems automatically feed the data into ATS.

ATS assesses and presents these data for every cargo shipment, including containerized shipments and bulk shipments.[23] For containerized shipments, a single shipment may consist of one or more containers, or multiple shipments may be consolidated into a single container for transport. Because ATS collects and presents data on shipments, CBP targets shipments—rather than individual containers—for examination. For a shipment that includes multiple containers, CBP may select some containers to examine or may examine all the containers in the shipment. If a targeted shipment is packed into a container with other shipments, CBP may examine the entire container.[24]

ATS performs a risk-based assessment of cargo shipments that CBP uses to focus its resources for conducting examinations and enhance its ability to identify potential violations of U.S. law, possible terrorist threats, and other threats to border security. To do so, ATS incorporates two types of targeting rules—strategic and tactical—to identify risk factors in shipment data.

- **Strategic rules:** Rules that identify general intelligence or threats or that identify relationships among different data elements within a single record or across multiple records. The process to update strategic rules involves iterations of testing to ensure that rules have their intended effect.
- **Tactical rules:** Rules that identify risks posed by specific intelligence or threats and are typically based on specific entries for one or more shipment data elements. Tactical rules can generally be updated in time to react to specific intelligence.

ATS has many rules, and one set of rules within ATS is programmed to check for information or patterns that could be indicative of suspicious or terrorist activity. This set of rules is referred to collectively as the maritime national security weight set (the weight set) because each rule in the set has a specific weight value assigned to it, and for each risk factor that rules identify, the weight values are added together to calculate an overall risk score for the shipment. For example, some rules in the weight set determine if any of the supply chain parties have possible matches to known terrorists or previous violations of U.S. law, and other rules in the weight set evaluate the completeness of the data, for example, whether addresses are provided as required for supply chain parties listed in the data, such as the importer. The weight set includes both strategic and tactical rules.

CBP classifies the risk scores from the weight set as low, medium, or high risk. Shipments with connections to known or suspected terrorists as well as those that include invalid information are more likely to be classified as high risk, and shipments from trusted shippers who participate in CBP's Customs-Trade Partnership Against Terrorism are more likely to be classified as low risk.

CBP can make updates to the weight set when the need arises. According to CBP, some updates, such as responding to specific intelligence information, can be implemented in a short amount of time. Substantial updates to the weight set, such as integrating the 10+2 rule data, can take longer to develop and implement. As part of this process, CBP may add new rules, change existing rules, or adjust the weights assigned to rules. To make such substantial updates to the weight set, CBP uses a multistep process that includes (1) identifying new requirements, (2) designing alternative versions of the weight set that may address the new requirements in different ways, (3) testing and evaluating those alternative versions, (4) selecting and implementing the new version to replace the existing version of the weight set, and (5) monitoring the performance of the new version of the weight set after implementation. According to CBP's Rules Development Concept of Operations, which describes the processes for updating the weight set, a substantial update provides the opportunity for a full assessment and evaluation of alternatives before CBP implements a new version of the weight set. CBP completed the most recent substantial update to the weight set in early 2011.[25]

National Security Targeting Responsibilities within CBP

Within CBP, targeters are stationed at different locations with varying responsibilities and focuses depending on their location, as described below.

- **Container Security Initiative ports:** CBP places targeters at designated foreign ports to work with their foreign counterparts to identify shipments that may pose a high risk for containing WMD or other terrorist contraband before the shipments are loaded onto U.S.-bound vessels.[26] When CBP targeters at a Container Security Initiative port determine through advance information that a U.S.- bound cargo shipment poses a high risk, CBP typically requests that the host government scan the container(s) with radiation detection and NII equipment. If these scans indicate the potential presence of WMD or other contraband, CBP is to request that the host government conduct a physical inspection of the shipment. If the host government declines, CBP can either issue a "do not load" order to prevent the shipment from being loaded onto a U.S.-bound vessel or flag the shipment for further examination upon arrival at the domestic port.
- **Advance Targeting Units (ATU):** ATUs are located at select domestic ports, and their targeting efforts are focused on shipments destined for ports within their respective regions. An ATU may be responsible for targeting shipments arriving at multiple ports in a region. For example, targeters at the Port of Houston are also responsible for targeting shipments that are bound for Freeport, Texas. CBP targeters at ATUs can review data as soon as carriers and importers submit the required data in accordance with the 24- hour

rule and the 10+2 rule, and the data are available in ATS. After reviewing the data, if the shipment data indicate a substantial risk that cannot be mitigated through an overseas examination at a Container Security Initiative port or by obtaining additional information about the shipment through additional research, the targeters may seek approval for a “do not load” order from the NTC-C Director before a shipment is loaded onto a U.S.-bound vessel. Once a shipment is loaded onto a vessel, targeters continue to review shipment data in ATS and use other sources, such as public records, to assess whether the shipment could pose a risk, in which case a targeter may target the shipment for examination upon arrival.

- **NTC-C:** In contrast to targeters at Container Security Initiative ports and ATUs, who focus their reviews on those shipments that are transiting from or to their respective ports, targeters at NTC-C review shipments for security risks from a national perspective. For example, if there is specific intelligence regarding an attempt to smuggle a terrorist weapon in a container, NTC-C targeters can use ATS to identify whether any shipments destined for the United States match the intelligence information, regardless of the port of arrival. NTC-C targeters also serve as a resource for other CBP targeters stationed at foreign and domestic ports because targeters at NTC-C may have access to research tools, such as classified databases, that may not be available to CBP targeters at these other locations.

CBP Uses ATS and Other Tools to Target Maritime Cargo Shipments for National Security Purposes

ATS is the primary system that CBP targeters use to review maritime cargo shipments for national security purposes, and targeters we spoke with were generally satisfied with how ATS and its weight set of national security rules have assisted in their targeting efforts. For example, targeters at one ATU we visited said that because ATS filters information and presents key information to the targeters, the targeters are able to better focus their targeting efforts than before they had ATS.[27] Those targeters as well as the ATU supervisor at another ATU noted that, in particular, the risk scores that the current version of the weight set produces are helpful in balancing their targeting workload. The risk score, however, is not the sole factor that determines whether a targeter reviews the data for a shipment or whether the shipment is selected for a security examination. In particular, targeters at each of the six ATUs we visited explained that they use the ATS risk score as a starting point for the targeting process, but that their decisions are ultimately based on additional research. To conduct this research, they may use information within ATS or other tools and information outside of ATS. On the basis of the ATS risk score and the research conducted, targeters make a qualitative assessment of the risk and determine whether to hold a shipment for examination. Targeters at one of the ATUs we visited emphasized the important role that targeters' expertise and experience play in the risk assessment process, stating that although they believe ATS's capabilities are helpful, they believe that there could be negative effects from further automating the targeting process, such as decreased use of targeters' expertise regarding the different types of shipments that arrive at their respective ports.[28]

According to CBP policy, the risk scores assigned by the weight set in ATS determine, in part, what actions CBP officers at the ports are to take to address potential threats. Targeters at ATUs are required to review data in ATS for all medium-risk and high-risk shipments that arrive at their respective ports. For example, a targeter may review individual data elements, such as the name of the importer or other supply chain parties. A targeter may also review the rules that detected potential threats and, therefore, contributed to the calculation of the risk score.[29] ATU targeters are also required to hold high-risk shipments for examination unless they can mitigate the risk through additional research or analysis of available information.[30] CBP targeters at each of the six ATUs we visited demonstrated how they implement this policy at their respective ports. In addition to actions targeters take in accordance with CBP policy, targeters have discretion over which low-risk and medium-risk shipments to select for security examinations, and CBP expects targeters to select shipments based on discretionary factors.[31]

Targeters use various features within ATS to assist them in their research into shipments of interest. Officials at each of the six ATUs we visited discussed or demonstrated the following features and how targeters use these features when targeting:

- **Queries:** Through ATS's querying capabilities, targeters are able to search for shipments that meet specific criteria, such as shipments from a particular country. For example, targeters at each ATU we visited use queries to identify shipments for review, although the set of queries used varied at each ATU. Five of the six ATUs we visited use queries to ensure that all shipments, regardless of risk score, are reviewed prior to arrival. For example, targeters at one ATU run a query for each arriving vessel to ensure that all shipments on the vessel have been reviewed. Targeters at another ATU have a query for each risk level (high, medium, or low) and targeters reviewing the results of each query are to ensure that all shipments of a particular risk level have been reviewed. In addition, targeters at five of the six ATUs we visited said that they run additional queries of interest for discretionary targeting after completing their assigned duties. Such discretionary targeting could be for national security purposes or for other efforts, such as counternarcotics. For example, targeters at one ATU may independently create queries to identify items of interest, such as all shipments of a particular commodity or those coming from a particular country of origin. In addition to queries that targeters at the ATUs run, NTC-C targeters run nationwide queries daily to identify shipments with the potential for containing chemical, biological, radiological, nuclear, or conventional weapons, among other things.

- **Targeters' notes:** ATS has a feature that allows a targeter to annotate a shipment with the targeter's conclusion based on research regarding whether the shipment is considered a potential threat. The notes feature within ATS facilitates the sharing of research findings with CBP targeters at other locations.
- **Targeters' reviews:** ATS also indicates whether the shipment data have been reviewed by a targeter at the targeter's own location or at another CBP targeting location, such as a Container Security Initiative port or NTC-C.

CBP targeters also use tools outside of ATS to conduct research. During our interviews at the six domestic port ATUs we visited, targeters explained that they use web-based and other research tools to aid in their assessments of shipments. Such tools include web searches, which targeters use to find general information on a company or address; a third-party database of public and proprietary records, which targeters use to research business names and associated information such as a business's locations, officers, and assets (e.g., registered vehicles); and the State Department's Consular Consolidated Database, which targeters may use to obtain visa and passport information for foreign individuals involved in a shipment. Targeters review and analyze all of

the information collected to make a decision as to whether a shipment should be examined. On the basis of such research and analysis, a targeter could select a low-risk shipment for examination. A targeter could also determine that an examination is not necessary for a medium-risk shipment—for example, the weight set may assign a medium-risk score to a shipment based on the data available, but the targeter could determine through research that the score is based on a clerical error in the data provided.

Targeters' experience may also inform targeting decisions. For example, targeters at ATUs may have information about recent seizures and can look for recurring patterns to identify future shipments that may be part of a trend of illegal shipments. Targeters may also share such information with other targeting units to help inform targeting decisions. Also, targeters at all six of the ATUs we visited said they communicate regularly with targeters at NTC-C regarding shipments of interest.

CBP's Efforts to Assess the Weight Set Have Been Limited

CBP Developed Performance Measures to Assess the Weight Set but Is Continuing to Update the Methodology

We have previously reported that ensuring controls to assess ATS's effectiveness in identifying high-risk shipments was important for providing CBP with the best information to inform its targeting efforts.[32] In 2005, in response to our work and an external peer review[33] of ATS conducted in 2005, CBP contracted with a consulting firm to develop performance measures and a methodology to determine the effectiveness of the weight set in identifying high-risk shipments. The resulting performance measures and methodology, which the consulting firm provided to CBP in April 2006, balanced targeting accuracy with examination workload and enabled CBP to compare the weight set's performance with the effectiveness of examinations conducted through a random selection program. We then reported in August 2006 that the performance measures and methodology developed by the consulting firm were sufficient to assess the performance of the weight set and provide a baseline against which future assessments may be conducted;[34] however, we also reported that data limitations and uncertainties existed, and we noted that CBP must interpret the evaluations cautiously.[35] We also reported in August

2006 that CBP planned to continue using the consulting firm's methodology in making future adjustments to the weight set. For more information about GAO's past audit findings and recommendations to improve the targeting process, see appendix II.

Currently, CBP assesses the performance of the weight set using the following performance measures:

- **True positive rate (TPR)** which reflects the percentage of maritime shipments that ATS assessed as high risk within the population of shipments in which CBP identified a threat during an examination.
- **False positive rate (FPR)** which reflects the percentage of maritime shipments that ATS assessed as high risk within the population of shipments in which CBP did not identify a threat during an examination.

Taken in combination, the TPR and FPR measures enable CBP to determine the effectiveness of the weight set by providing information about the accuracy of the weight set and its impact on examination workload. The TPR enables CBP to determine the accuracy of the weight set in identifying high-risk shipments. The TPR and FPR measures also enable CBP to determine the workload or examination rate for ports based on the results of the weight set scores. For example, a high FPR would unnecessarily increase the workload or number of examinations at ports because officials would be required to examine a higher number of shipments that do not contain an actual threat. Using data from the version of the weight set CBP was using in 2005, the consulting firm used its methodology to conduct a performance assessment, which involved calculating the TPR and FPR to ultimately indicate the effectiveness of the weight set at that time. Since the contract with the firm ended in 2011, CBP has taken on the role of assessing the effectiveness of the weight set. In its project plan for the most recent update to the weight set implemented in early 2011, as it had previously done, CBP planned to assess the performance using these measures to compare the targeting effectiveness of the weight set with other measurements.

CBP officials stated that they face ongoing challenges with the performance measures and the methodology by which they are calculated. In particular, the FPR and TPR may not accurately reflect the weight set's performance in identifying national security threats because they rely on indirect measures given that no true security threat has been found in a cargo container. We reported in 2006 that CBP planned to take steps to improve the process for assessing ATS performance. Since the most recent update to the weight set in early 2011, CBP formed working groups and has begun taking steps to ensure that the methodology it uses to approximate threats accurately reflects what CBP considers to be a national security threat (to the extent possible). For example, these working groups plan to (1) create a new definition of "national security" for the purposes of clarifying what the weight set should target and (2) revisit the current definitions of threats in containers to provide consistency with the new definition of national security. CBP officials stated that they expect the working groups' activities to be completed by April 2013.

CBP Does Not Have Reasonable Assurance That the Updated Weight Set Is More Effective than Alternative Versions or the Version It Replaced

Prior to implementing the current version of the weight set in early 2011, CBP did not conduct an assessment to determine whether the updated version of the weight set would be more effective than the previous version of the weight set or other alternatives that were considered during the update process. For the 2011 update, CBP developed and evaluated five alternative versions of the weight set. CBP's consideration for which alternative to select focused on two of the five versions because, according to CBP officials, these two versions incorporated the newly required 10+2 data and reflected current threat information about countries of interest. CBP ultimately implemented one of these two versions of the weight set, but CBP could not provide any documentation to demonstrate that the version selected was more effective than either the other alternative or the version it was to replace.

CBP's process for updating the weight set involves assessing the impact of alternative versions of the weight set. For example, for the most recent update to the weight set, CBP's impact assessment provides information on how many shipments would be assessed as high risk under each alternative version of the weight set and would, therefore, affect CBP targeters' workload at ports of arrival because such high-risk shipments, under CBP policy, are to be held for examination, for example, through the use of NII equipment. CBP officials stated that they believed the impact assessment that CBP conducted during the update process indicates the reasons for selecting the chosen version of the weight set.

While, according to CBP officials, the impact assessment provides CBP's reason for replacing the prior version of the weight set, we found that the impact assessment primarily evaluates how the chosen alternative version of the weight set could affect targeter workload and does not address measures of accuracy in identifying high-risk shipments. Therefore, the impact assessment does not fully account for the effectiveness of each alternative of the weight set. Although managing resources is an element of risk management, effectiveness in reducing risks is also an important consideration when evaluating alternatives to manage risk. CBP's impact assessment does not address the balance between targeting accuracy and workload.

Assessing the potential effectiveness of alternative versions of the weight set prior to selecting one for implementation would provide CBP with more information to make an informed decision. In January 2010, the DHS Office of Inspector General recommended that CBP enhance its documentation efforts to ensure that each stage of the process for analyzing and developing ATS rules is documented, and CBP concurred with this recommendation.[36] As part of this recommendation, the DHS Office of Inspector General recommended documenting the rationale for making changes to ATS rules but did not specify what types of analyses could demonstrate or support the rationale for making changes to the rules. On the basis of our analysis, the rationale for updates to the weight set could be further strengthened through assessments of effectiveness beyond workload. For example, determining the expected TPR and FPR for an alternative version of the weight set and comparing these measures against the TPR and FPR for the existing version of the weight set could enable CBP to determine if the alternative version of the weight set could be expected to result in improved effectiveness, based on these performance measures. This would enable CBP to quantitatively compare the effectiveness of the alternative versions of the weight set being considered prior to selecting one for implementation. Doing so, in addition to the impact assessment, would provide CBP with reasonable assurance that the version of the weight set it selects for implementation is the most effective of the alternatives considered after taking into account any resource constraints. Furthermore, assessing the alternative versions of the weight set in the future would provide CBP with better assurance that the version it selects for implementation is more effective than the previous version of the weight set. CBP officials stated that they plan to calculate and document measures of effectiveness during the planned update to the weight set that will begin in the fall of 2012.

CBP Has Not Regularly Assessed the Weight Set against Performance Targets to Determine when Updates Are Needed

Since implementing the current version of the weight set in early 2011, CBP has not regularly assessed the weight set against established performance targets to monitor its performance and obtain information to determine when updates to the weight set are necessary. We reported in August 2006 that CBP intended to establish targets for the performance measures to assess future performance of ATS, but CBP did not establish such targets for those measures.

Targets could help CBP determine when updates are needed to improve targeting effectiveness. For example, according to CBP's analysis, the TPR for summer 2011 through spring 2012 shows that, among shipments CBP found to contain a potential threat during an examination, the weight set accurately identified 6.3 percent as high risk, meaning that the weight set classified 93.7 percent of shipments that carried a potential threat as either medium risk or low risk. Furthermore, the FPR for that time period shows that, among all the arriving shipments that CBP examined during that time that did not pose a threat, the weight set identified 3.6 percent as high risk. However, because CBP did not establish targets for either TPR or FPR, it is not clear whether 6.3 percent for the TPR is sufficiently low or 3.6 percent for the FPR is sufficiently high to suggest that changes are needed to improve the performance of the weight set.

CBP's project plan calls for conducting periodic performance assessments by determining recurring measures of TPR and FPR. Furthermore, according to CBP officials, the performance assessments are to be conducted as part of quarterly reporting responsibilities. However, CBP did not calculate these measures at the end of each quarter, but instead calculated them as part of a single assessment in the summer of 2012 and divided the results into quarters.[37] Accordingly, CBP was not aware of the ongoing performance of the weight set from its implementation in early 2011 through spring 2012, and CBP was therefore unable to determine for 18 months whether the weight set was performing at a level that could require changes or updates to improve its effectiveness. According to CBP officials, the summer 2012 assessment was conducted at that time in preparation for a conference to discuss updates to the weight set planned for the fall of 2012. CBP had decided to hold this conference before CBP conducted the assessment, meaning its decision for when to update the weight set was not based on information about the weight set's effectiveness from ongoing monitoring of CBP's performance measures for the weight set.

Ongoing monitoring is a key element of a risk management approach, and CBP's project plan calls for such periodic performance monitoring to determine targeting effectiveness. In addition, standard practices for internal control indicate that (1) ongoing monitoring should occur in the course of normal operations and can be accomplished by periodic review of performance measures and (2) in the process of ongoing performance monitoring, actions should include continuous comparison of performance data against planned targets and analysis of any differences to take corrective actions as necessary.

CBP officials stated that personnel have not been consistently available to conduct performance assessments since the initial contract with the consulting firm ended in July 2011 and that resource concerns, such as funding, the availability of subject matter experts, and the availability of programmers may affect the timing of weight set updates. Nevertheless, given the importance of the weight set to CBP's process for targeting cargo containers, regular performance assessments of the weight set that include evaluating results against established performance targets could help CBP determine when updates are needed in a timelier manner and help it better prioritize the resources it needs to complete the updates.[38] Furthermore, CBP officials stated that they intend to continue adjusting the methodology for calculating the performance measures to mitigate data limitations and more accurately reflect the performance of the weight set. Such steps could help CBP ensure that its targeters have the best information available regarding the risk of maritime cargo container shipments arriving in the United States.

CONCLUSION

CBP recognizes the importance of and challenges to ensuring the security of the global supply chain while facilitating the flow of legitimate commerce. Although no events have occurred to date, terror-related attacks on the supply chain could have devastating effects on the nation's security and economic well-being, and it is imperative that CBP use the best information and tools available to continually mitigate potential threats and address vulnerabilities. DHS and CBP face difficulties in achieving 100 percent scanning of cargo containers prior to loading at foreign ports and have, instead, advocated a risk-based approach to target and scan those cargo containers that pose the highest risk. Given the critical role that ATS plays as part of this risk-based approach, it is important to ensure that ATS is performing effectively.

CBP plans to continue enhancing risk management processes, including the use of ATS and its associated targeting rules. CBP's determination of which containerized shipments to review or to hold for examination is based, in part, on the risk score. Thus, updating the weight set in ATS that calculates this risk score is important for ensuring that targeters are using the most effective tools in making targeting decisions. CBP has assessed workload impacts when making updates to the weight set, but it did not fully assess the weight set's effectiveness as part of the most recent update. As a result, CBP does not have reasonable assurance that the implemented version is the most effective. Further, CBP did not conduct periodic assessments as part of ongoing monitoring efforts. Specifically, CBP did not conduct an assessment of the weight set until 18 months after CBP implemented the new weight set. We believe it is important that CBP more regularly assess the performance of the weight set in ATS that produces the risk scores and compare the results of this assessment against established performance targets. Such steps could help CBP determine when changes may be needed and ensure that its targeters have the best information available regarding the risk of maritime cargo container shipments arriving in the United States.

Recommendations for Executive Action

To enhance its targeting of maritime cargo containers and better position CBP to provide reasonable assurance of the effectiveness of ATS, we recommend that the Commissioner of CBP take the following two actions:

- ensure that future updates to the weight set are based on results of assessments that demonstrate that the chosen version of the weight set is more effective than other alternatives, including the existing version, and
- establish targets for CBP's performance measures and use those measures to assess the effectiveness of the weight set on a regular basis to better determine when updates to the weight set are needed.

AGENCY COMMENTS

On October 17, 2012, DHS provided written comments on a draft of this report. DHS concurred with the two recommendations. Specifically, DHS concurred with the recommendation to ensure that future updates to the weight set are based on the results of assessments and stated that CBP plans to conduct analyses to ensure that future versions of the weight set result in increased effectiveness. DHS also noted that CBP is to conduct these analyses during the development and deployment of future versions of the weight set. According to DHS, these analyses would include performance measures, subject matter expert input, current threat information, and other intelligence. DHS stated that it expects these actions to be completed by April 2013. Such actions should address the intent of the recommendation to ensure improvements in the effectiveness of future versions of the weight set. DHS also concurred with the recommendation to establish targets for CBP's performance measures and stated that CBP is working to improve the current performance measures methodology. DHS stated that, following approval of this methodology, CBP plans to conduct quarterly reviews of the weight set to inform decision making. DHS stated that it expects these actions to be completed by September 2013. If CBP takes these steps as planned and includes targets for any performance measures that are part of the updated methodology, this should address the intent of our recommendation. DHS also provided technical comments, which we incorporated as appropriate.

Stephen L. Caldwell
Director
Homeland Security and Justice

APPENDIX I: FEDERAL STRATEGY FOR ENSURING THE SECURITY OF MARITIME CARGO CONTAINER SHIPMENTS

This appendix describes the core programs related to U.S. Customs and Border Protection's (CBP) strategy for ensuring the security of maritime cargo container shipments. CBP has developed this strategy to mitigate the risk of weapons of mass destruction, terrorist-related material, or other contraband being smuggled into the United States in cargo containers. CBP's strategy is based on related programs that attempt to focus resources on potentially risky cargo shipped in containers while allowing other cargo containers to proceed without unduly disrupting commerce into the United States. The strategy includes obtaining advanced cargo information to identify high-risk containers, using technology to inspect cargo containers, and partnering with foreign governments and the trade industry. Table 1 provides a brief description of the core programs that compose this security strategy.

Table 1. Description of CBP's Core Cargo Security Programs

Program and year introduced	Description
Obtaining advanced information to identify high-risk containers	
Automated Targeting System (ATS), 1999	ATS is an intranet-based enforcement and decision support system that compares traveler, cargo, and conveyance information against intelligence and other enforcement data by incorporating risk-based targeting scenarios and assessments. ATS assigns a risk score to arriving cargo shipments based on shipping information to help CBP identify and prevent potential terrorists and terrorist weapons from entering the United States.
24-hour rule, 2002	CBP generally requires vessel carriers to electronically transmit cargo manifests to CBP's Automated Manifest System 24 hours before U.S.-bound cargo is loaded onto a vessel at a foreign port. The information is used by ATS in its calculation of risk scores. The cargo manifest information is submitted by vessel carriers for all arriving cargo shipments.
Importer Security Filing and Additional Carrier Requirements (also known as 10+2), 2009	CBP requires importers and vessel carriers to provide data elements for improved identification of containerized shipments that may pose a risk for terrorism. The importer is responsible for supplying CBP with 10 shipping data elements, such as country of origin, 24 hours prior to loading, while the vessel carrier is required to provide two data elements, container status messages and stow plans, not required by the 24-hour rule.[a]
Domestic scanning technology deployments	
Nonintrusive inspection (NII) equipment, 2001	CBP uses NII equipment to actively scan both randomly selected containers and those identified by ATS as high risk. NII uses X-rays or gamma rays to scan a container and create images of the container's contents without opening it. According to CBP, as of August 2012, it had deployed 93 NII systems to U.S. portsto scan containers. In fiscal year 2011, CBP scanned 4.13 percent of containers arriving at U.S. ports.
Radiation portal monitors, 2002	CBP's program to scan 100 percent of containers arriving in the United States with radiation detection equipment prior to leaving a domestic port. As of July 2012, DHS had deployed 447 radiation portal monitors at U.S. seaports, through which approximately 99 percent of all containers arriving by sea pass.

Table 1. (Continued)

Program and year introduced	Description
Container Security Initiative, 2002	CBP places staff at participating foreign ports to work with host country customs officials to target and examine high-risk container cargo for weapons of mass destruction before they are shipped to the United States. CBP officials identify the containers that may pose a risk for terrorism and request that their foreign counterparts examine the contents of the containers.
Secure Freight Initiative, 2006	CBP and the Department of Energy initiated this program at selected ports to scan 100 percent of U.S.-bound container cargo for nuclear and radiological materials overseas using integrated examination systems that couple NII and radiation detection equipment. Since its inception, all but one of the selected ports has reverted to Container Security Initiative operations.
Customs-Trade Partnership Against Terrorism, 2001	CBP develops voluntary partnerships with members of the international trade community composed of importers; manufacturers; customs brokers; forwarders; air,sea, and land carriers; and contract logistics providers. Private companies that implement specific security measures and best practices receive facilitated processing, such as a reduced likelihood of security-based examinations of their cargo.
Mutual recognition arrangements, various years[b]	Through mutual recognition arrangements with other countries, the security-related practices and programs taken by the customs administration of one country are recognized and accepted by the administration of another. According to CBP, the essential concept is that the Customs-Trade Partnership Against Terrorism and the foreign programs are compatible in both theory and practice so that one program may recognize the findings and validation results provided by another.

Source: GAO summary of information provided by DHS.

[a] Container Status Messages report terminal container movements, such as loading and discharging the vessel, and report the change in the status of containers, such as if they are empty or full. The stow plan contains the position of each cargo container on a vessel.

[b] These mutual recognition arrangements were individually negotiated and signed in different years. CBP has signed arrangements with New Zealand (2007), Canada (2008), Jordan (2008), Japan (2009), Korea (2010), and the European Union (2012).

Appendix II: Past Audit Findings and Recommendations to Improve the Targeting Process

Since 2004, we have conducted audits of CBP's targeting process and ATS. In particular, we published reports related to these topics in February

2004, August 2006, and September 2010.[1] In addition, the Coast Guard and Maritime Transportation Act of 2004 requires the Department of Homeland Security's (DHS) Office of Inspector General (OIG) to report annually on its evaluation of the current targeting system for international intermodal cargo containers.[2] Our and DHS OIG's audits have addressed, among other things, incorporating key elements of a risk management framework and recognized modeling practices, documenting the targeting rule development process, improving data collection and ATS's use of data, and providing additional information outside of ATS to targeters. Collectively, these audits have made recommendations to DHS and CBP for improving the targeting process, and CBP has taken actions to implement them, although in some cases CBP's implementation efforts have been slow, leaving CBP without the benefits of these improvements for several years. This appendix provides an overview of key findings and recommendations from these audits, as well as the status of actions taken to implement the recommendations.[3]

Incorporating Key Elements of a Risk Management Framework and Recognized Modeling Practices

In February 2004, we reported that while CBP had taken steps to address the terrorism risks posed by maritime cargo containers, its targeting strategy did not incorporate all key elements of a risk management framework, and ATS was not consistent with certain recognized modeling practices. We recommended, among other things, that CBP improve the targeting strategy by incorporating key elements of a risk management framework and recognized modeling practices. These recommendations included specific steps CBP should take to help ensure it could achieve the objectives of its overall targeting strategy and better ensure that the tools it uses to protect against terrorism are working effectively at the nation's ports. We later reported, in August 2006, that CBP had made progress addressing the recommendations but had not yet fully implemented the recommendations in our February 2004 report.[4] Since that time, CBP has fully implemented the February 2004 recommendations aimed at improving the targeting strategy by incorporating key elements of a risk management framework and recognized modeling practices. Table 2 provides more detail on our February 2004 recommendations and CBP's efforts to implement them.

Table 2. Status of GAO Recommendations from February 2004

Recommended steps for incorporating key elements of a risk management framework and recognized modeling practices	Status of the recommendation
Conduct and use a comprehensive set of threat, criticality, vulnerability, and risk assessments related to maritime cargo containers to determine the need for risk mitigation actions	**Implemented** In August 2006, we reported that CBP was conducting risk assessments based on threat and intelligence information it was receiving. Although CBP was preparing threat assessments, it did not have a documented methodology in place to guide its personnel in identifying sources of threat information, what approach to take in conducting the assessment, and key elements to include that could help ensure consistency in the preparation of such assessments. As a result, we made an additional recommendation inAugust 2006 related to establishing and documenting a methodology for conducting threat assessments, which CBP subsequently implemented in October 2006.
Initiate an external peer review of ATS to evaluate, among other things, the types and sources of data being used and the appropriateness and weighting of targeting rules	**Implemented** In response to this recommendation, CBP contracted with a consulting firm in 2005 and 2006 to conduct a peer review and to develop performance measures, obtain additional insights into ATS's performance, and determine whether ATS is more effective at targeting shipments than a random sampling approach.
Implement a mandatory random sampling program that cannot be waived, which would allow CBP to better compare the inspection results from its random sample program with those of ATS, and which may result in improvements to the targeting rules.[a]	**Implemented** CBP's Compliance Measurement Program randomly selects shipments based on customs entry information submitted by the trade industry. We reviewed CBP's sampling methodology and determined that its sampling techniques support a statistically valid random probability sample. In August 2006 we reported that CBP had made progress in conducting random sampling, but that at the time, CBP was unable to compare the examination results from its Compliance Measurement Program with ATS inspection results because CBP did not yet have an automated system in place to compare multiple sets of data—like results of random examinations with results of routine ATS inspections.Subsequently, in March 2008, CBP implemented the Cargo Enforcement Reporting and Tracking System (CERTS) within ATS to capture examination findings.[b] As a result of its actions, CBP is better positioned to systematically analyze inspection results for adjusting ATS.

Recommended steps for incorporating key elements of a risk management framework and recognized modeling practices	Status of the recommendation
Conduct simulated events to operationally test and validate the targeting strategy	**Implemented** We reported in August 2006 that CBP had not yet conducted simulated events such as covert tests and computer-generated simulations to test and validate the effectiveness of ATS in targeting oceangoing cargo shipped in containers that pose the highest risk of having links to terrorism. CBP has since taken actions to implement this recommendation by, among other things, developing and implementing a testing and simulation environment to conduct computer-generated tests of ATS. In June 2007, CBP reported to us that as of May 2007, it had tested approximately 26,000 mock cargo shipments and modified or updated information contained in ATS.
Monitor and evaluate the effectiveness of risk mitigation actions taken so that the targeting strategy may be amended as needed and responds to changes in risk	**Implemented** CBP contracted a consulting firm to develop performance measures, and the consulting firm produced a report in April 2006 that outlined performance measures and a methodology for assessing the effectiveness of ATS. CBP has continued to use these performance measures, but as we have stated in this report, CBP's assessments of ATS's effectiveness have not occurred on a regular basis.

Source: GAO.

[a]In addition to this recommendation, the DHS OIG made a recommendation in July 2005 that CBP use examination results to refine ATS targeting rules. See DHS OIG, *Audit of Targeting Oceangoing Cargo Containers (Unclassified Summary)*, OIG-05-26 (Washington, D.C.: July 2005).

[b]The DHS OIG recommended in August 2007 that CBP develop systematic procedures to extract oceangoing container examination results information and begin using it to refine existing targeting rules and developing new rules. DHS OIG stated in its report that the intention of its recommendation was satisfied as CBP had plans for and had begun implementing CERTS. This August 2007 DHS OIG report contains sensitive information and is therefore not publicly available. The DHS OIG subsequently issued a report in June 2008 with recommendations related to the management and oversight of the development and implementation of CERTS. See DHS OIG, *Targeting of Cargo Containers 2008: Review of CBP's Cargo Enforcement Reporting and Tracking System*, OIG-08-65 (Washington, D.C.: Jun. 11, 2008). As noted above in the table, CBP fully implemented CERTS in May 2008.

In August 2006, among other things, we reported on the status of recommendations issued in our February 2004 report and reiterated the importance of the recommendations. Additionally, with respect to the recommendation regarding risk assessments, at the time, CBP had begun taking action to implement the recommendation by conducting and using risk assessments that incorporated discussions of potential threats and estimates of the relative importance of assets and vulnerabilities associated with the supply chain. We noted, though, that CBP did not have a methodology in place to guide its staff in identifying sources of threat information, such as agencies to contact, what approach to take in conducting the assessment, and key elements to include that would help ensure consistency in the preparation of threat assessments associated with the movement of cargo shipped in containers. As a result, we further recommended that CBP establish and document a methodology for conducting threat assessments associated with cargo shipped in containers to help ensure that CBP staff responsible for conducting threat assessments consult relevant information sources, prepare threat assessments consistently, and include key elements to effectively communicate risk to program managers.

In response to that recommendation, in October 2006, CBP issued a protocol to assist its intelligence research specialists in preparing port threat assessments in support of the Container Security Initiative. Under this initiative, CBP places staff at foreign seaports to work with foreign counterparts to inspect high-risk containers before they are shipped to the United States. The October 2006 protocol included a discussion of information sources for CBP staff to consult and the overall methodology to follow in making the port threat assessment. CBP also distributed a template that discussed the key elements its specialists should include when preparing port threat assessments. In addition, CBP developed a checklist for its specialists to use to help ensure that appropriate information sources are consulted in making port threat assessments. To assist in addressing threats related to global supply chain logistics and the movement of maritime containers carrying cargo arriving in the United States, CBP established an Office of Intelligence and Operations Coordination in October 2007, which has since been renamed the Office of Intelligence and Investigative Liaison. This office includes the Analysis and Targeting Division (A&T), which is composed of program managers with operational experience and intelligence analysts and is responsible for conducting risk assessments of countries (known as country risk profiles) that consider threats, vulnerabilities, and the associated criticality of related assets from which or through which cargo is shipped to the United

States. In 2008, the A&T Division assessed risks in two primary mission areas: (1) terrorism and weapons of mass destruction and (2) narcotics. On the basis of these assessments, the A&T Division developed a risk assessment methodology to rank countries according to the level of risk associated with each mission area. The A&T Division teams translated these rankings into scores, and program managers integrated them into ATS. Specifically, CBP integrated the rankings for the terrorism mission into ATS in 2008 and for the narcotics mission in 2009. Thus, CBP has fully addressed this recommendation and is better positioned to ensure consistency in the preparation of risk assessments associated with the movement of maritime cargo container shipments.

Documenting the Targeting Rule Development Process

In January 2010, the DHS OIG reported on several aspects of CBP's process for developing and updating targeting rules in ATS.[5] In this report, the DHS OIG stated that CBP could improve its process for changing or deleting targeting rules by, among other things, documenting (1) rule change decisions and (2) the testing and evaluation of rule changes. Specifically, one component of the rule update process involves the review of the proposed rule changes by subject matter experts, and the DHS OIG reported that CBP could improve the process by ensuring the rationale for changes implemented or not implemented are documented and recorded for future use. Furthermore, the DHS OIG reported that CBP tested new rules using actual data to determine how well the new rules are working, but the DHS OIG noted that this process for testing and evaluating the rules, and subsequent modifications of the new rules, was not documented. The DHS OIG recommended that CBP ensure it documents each stage of the process for analyzing and developing ATS rules, including the rationale for making changes and the details on tools used to improve application consistency and rule change standardization. According to the DHS OIG report, in response to this recommendation, CBP (1) developed a documentation process to capture and record information that includes the rationale for rule changes and the utilization of tools and (2) introduced more formality into the rules process by implementing a structure to guide national conferences, rule evaluation, targeting development, and process management, among other things. The DHS OIG stated in its report that it considered the actions taken by CBP to be responsive to the recommendation.

Improving Data Collection and ATS's Use of Data

In February 2004, in addition to making the recommendations discussed earlier, we also reported that CBP was relying on the manifest as its principal data input, and CBP did not mandate the transmission of additional information before a cargo's risk level was assigned. We reported that terrorism experts, members of the international trade community, and CBP inspectors at the ports we visited as part of that review characterized the ship's manifest as one of the least reliable or useful types of information for targeting purposes. We reported that terrorism experts, trade community representatives, and some CBP inspectors at ports we visited told us that CBP should explore requiring more timely electronic transmittal of additional data elements for cargo container targeting purposes, such as stowage plans (a map of where each container aboard a ship is stored), container movement tracking data, and entry data. Although we did not analyze the feasibility or the costs and benefits of these suggestions, we reported that it could be useful for CBP to explore requiring appropriate parties in the supply chain, such as the importer, to provide additional data elements for use in ATS to perform more complex linkage analyses and identify potential anomalies in the shipping documents filed. Although we did not make a recommendation directly related to data collection because we did not analyze the feasibility or the costs and benefits of collecting additional data, the recommendations in our report focused generally on incorporating key elements of recognized modeling practices, and one of the recognized modeling practices applicable to ATS is enhancing the sources and types of information input into ATS. Furthermore, in July 2005, the DHS OIG issued an unclassified summary of an audit regarding CBP's targeting for maritime cargo containers, which concluded that improvements were needed in the data to which ATS targeting rules are applied.[6]

In January 2009, CBP initiated an effort to collect additional data through the Importer Security Filing and Additional Carrier Requirements, collectively known as the 10+2 rule. The rule requires importers and carriers to provide 10 data elements and 2 data elements, respectively, to CBP for improving CBP's ability to identify high-risk cargo container shipments. Specifically, the 10+2 rule requires importers to submit information about the commodities being transported in a shipment and about entities involved in the supply chain. These additional data elements include information that we reported could be helpful in improving targeting efforts. In particular, the rule requires stowage plans and some elements of entry data. We reported in September 2010 that the 10+2 rule data elements were available for identifying high-risk cargo at that time, but that CBP had not yet updated ATS to fully incorporate the data into its targeting criteria.[7] We recommended that CBP establish milestones and time frames for updating the targeting criteria. In December 2010, CBP provided us with a project plan for integrating the data into its targeting criteria, and in early 2011, CBP implemented the updated targeting criteria to address risk factors present in the Importer Security Filing data.

Providing Additional Information Outside of ATS to Targeters

In November 2006, the DHS OIG reported on issues related to information that is available to targeters to conduct targeting activities.[8] The DHS OIG found that CBP targeters did not always have access to a particular system that directly accesses a database containing billions of records on individuals and businesses.

The DHS OIG recommended that CBP provide targeters with access to that system or a similar system that would allow targeters to access business records. In its report, the DHS OIG stated that it considered the recommendation to be implemented because CBP had acquired funding to grant personnel access to that system and had issued a memo stating that all personnel that were to be scheduled for targeting training should also have access to the system.[9]

The DHS OIG also found that it was unclear which personnel involved in targeting should have security clearances, and as a result, important information affecting container targeting and inspection decisions may not be available to the staff for making these decisions in a timely manner. The DHS OIG recommended that CBP increase the number of targeters with security clearances. In response to this recommendation, according to the DHS OIG, CBP presented a corrective action plan with an established completion date of June 30, 2007, for this recommendation. The DHS OIG further noted that in July 2006, CBP issued a memo for Security Clearance for Counter Terrorism Response Officers, directing CBP field offices to forward applications of port personnel that need to have security clearances. On the basis of these efforts, the DHS OIG reported that CBP had satisfied the intent of this recommendation.

End Notes

[1] U.S. Department of Transportation, Research and Innovative Technology Administration, Bureau of Transportation Statistics, *America's Container Ports: Linking Markets at Home and Abroad* (Washington, D.C.: January 2011).

[2] In addition to its priority mission of keeping terrorists and their weapons out of the United States, CBP is also responsible for securing the border, facilitating international trade and travel, collecting duties, and enforcing numerous U.S. laws and regulations pertaining to immigration and illicit drugs, among other things.

[3] Pub. L. No. 107-295, 116 Stat. 2064.

[4] See 46 U.S.C. § 70116.

[5] Pub. L. No. 109-347, 120 Stat. 1884.

[6] 6 U.S.C. § 981. A similar requirement was enacted that same year by the Department of Homeland Security Appropriations Act, 2007 (Pub. L. No. 109-295, 120 Stat. 1355 (2006)) and is codified at 6 U.S.C. § 981a. Both statutes specify scanning as examination with both radiation detection equipment and nonintrusive imaging equipment. 6 U.S.C. §§ 981(a), 981a(a)(1).

[7] Pub. L. No. 110-53, § 1701(a), 121 Stat. 266, 489-90 (amending 6 U.S.C. § 982(b)).

[8] Radiation detection equipment detects radiation being emitted from a container, and through an NII scan, CBP can identify anomalies in a container's image that could, among other things, indicate the presence of shielding material.

[9] The 9/11 Act scanning provision includes possible extensions for containers loaded at a port or ports for which DHS certifies that at least two out of a list of specific conditions exist. Among others, these conditions include the following: (1) adequate scanning equipment is not available or cannot be integrated with existing systems, (2) a port does not have the physical characteristics to install the equipment, or (3) use of the equipment will significantly affect trade capacity and the flow of cargo. See 6 U.S.C. § 982(b)(4).

[10] GAO, *Supply Chain Security: Container Security Programs Have Matured, but Uncertainty Persists over the Future of 100 Percent Scanning*, GAO-12-422T (Washington, D.C.: Feb. 7, 2012), and *Supply Chain Security: Feasibility and Cost-Benefit Analysis Would Assist DHS and Congress in Assessing and Implementing the Requirement to Scan 100 Percent of U.S.-Bound Containers*, GAO-10-12 (Washington, D.C.: Oct. 30, 2009).

[11] DHS, *Scanning of Maritime Cargo Containers: Fiscal Year 2012 Report to Congress* (Washington, D.C.: May 3, 2012).

[12] CBP refers to the automated process of analyzing data and classifying shipments by risk level as screening, and according to CBP, it screens (but does not scan) all U.S.-bound cargo shipments before they are loaded onto vessels at foreign ports. In this report, we discuss the screening process in terms of assessing the risk of a shipment. An examination refers to either (1) the scanning of a container or other cargo conveyance using large-scale NII technology, which may use X-rays or gamma rays to create an image of the contents of the container or other conveyance, or (2) a physical inspection of a container or other cargo conveyance. If the results of an NII scan indicate that a threat may be present, CBP may choose to conduct a physical inspection. In addition to an NII exam, scanning can also refer to the use of radiation detection equipment, such as radiation portal monitors. According to CBP, 99 percent of containers are scanned through radiation portal monitors prior to leaving a domestic port.

[13] In this report, we use the term "targeting" to refer to the synthesis and use of information from a variety of sources, including the results of screening, to identify shipments that may be a potential security risk.

[14] CBP collects data on the number of shipments as well as the number of containers arriving in the United States. A shipment is the tender of one lot of cargo at one time from one shipper to one recipient. In some cases, a shipment will refer to all the contents in a single container. In other cases, a shipment may refer to the cargo in multiple containers. Additionally, a single container could hold multiple shipments from different supply chain parties.

[15] We limited our selection to the 20 ports with the largest volume of arriving shipments in fiscal year 2011 because the consideration of our other criteria—specifically the percentage of high-risk or medium-risk shipments and the percentage of containers scanned using NII equipment—could be disproportionately influenced by ports with smaller volumes.

[16] According to CBP officials, prior to making an update to the weight set, CBP hosts a rules conference to discuss potential updates to the rules in the weight set. In February 2009, CBP hosted a conference (the Importer Security Filing rules conference) in which CBP officials explained policies regarding the receipt of new data from importers and vessel carriers and how the data were to be used in targeting. Targeters from various ports attended this conference as representatives of their ports and subject matter experts. According to CBP officials, this conference was different from rules conferences in the past. However, CBP could not provide attendee lists for the rules conference that preceded the Importer Security Filing conference, and therefore we used attendance at the Importer Security Filing conference as part of our criteria.

[17] NTC-C analyzes advance cargo tactical and strategic information using ATS before shipments reach the United States. NTC-C also promotes information sharing with other federal agencies and foreign governments to detect and seize threats at U.S. and foreign ports.

[18] DHS Office of Inspector General, *Cargo Targeting and Examinations*, OIG-10-34 (Washington, D.C.: Jan. 6, 2010). Because the reports we issued in February 2004 and August 2006 regarding CBP's targeting practices contain sensitive information, they are not publicly available.

[19] GAO, *Standards for Internal Control in the Federal Government*, GAO/AIMD-00-21.3.1 (Washington, D.C.: November 1999). These standards, issued pursuant to the requirements of the Federal Managers' Financial Integrity Act of 1982 (FMFIA), provide the overall framework for establishing and maintaining internal control in the federal government. Also pursuant to FMFIA, the Office of Management and Budget (OMB) issued Circular A-123, revised December 21, 2004, to provide the specific requirements for assessing the reporting on internal controls. Internal control standards, and the definition of internal control in OMB Circular A-123, are based on GAO's *Standards for Internal Control in the Federal Government.*

[20] 19 C.F.R. § 4.7(b). Cargo manifests are prepared by the ocean carrier and are composed of bills of lading for each shipment loaded onto a vessel to describe the contents of the shipments. Bills of lading are documents issued by a carrier describing the goods, the details of the intended voyage, and the conditions of transportation.

[21] Importer Security Filing and Additional Carrier Requirements, 73 *Fed. Reg.* 71,730 (Nov. 25, 2008) (codified at 19 C.F.R. pts. 4, 12, 18, 101, 103, 113, 122, 123, 141, 143, 149, 178, & 192).

[22] Container status messages report terminal container movements, such as loading and discharging the vessel, and report the change in the status of containers, such as if they are empty or full. Container status messages also report conveyance movements, such as vessel

arrivals and departures. A vessel stow plan includes information such as the vessel operator, voyage number, the stow position of each container, hazardous material code (if applicable), and the port of discharge.

[23] Bulk cargo is shipped loose in the hold of a ship, not in packages or containers. For example, grain, coal, oil, and chemicals are usually bulk cargo. Manifest data for bulk cargo must be submitted electronically to CBP 24 hours prior to arrival in the United States, rather than 24 hours prior to cargo being loaded onto U.S.-bound vessels at foreign ports, as is required for containerized cargo. See 19 C.F.R. § 4.7(b)(4).

[24] Examinations using NII equipment are conducted on containers (i.e., the resulting image from the exam will depict all contents of the container). If the examination includes a physical inspection, CBP may focus its efforts on the portion of the container that holds the targeted shipment.

[25] In February 2009, CBP convened a conference of subject matter experts, including targeters at domestic ports, to discuss integrating the 10+2 rule data into the weight set. Following the conference, CBP designed and evaluated five alternative versions of the weight set. In early 2011, CBP selected one of these alternative versions and implemented it, making it the current version of the weight set that CBP targeters use in their targeting efforts.

[26] The Container Security Initiative has been operational at 58 foreign ports since fiscal year 2007.

[27] CBP introduced ATS in 1999.

[28] We have previously reported similar findings related to CBP's targeting for intellectual property violations. In particular, we reported in April 2007 that CBP officials at several ports we visited expressed the view that there is no substitute for the skills and experience of a well-trained CBP officer; however, other officials noted that automated systems can assist with targeting because they can better handle data for vast volumes of shipments. For more information, see GAO, *Intellectual Property: Better Data Analysis and Integration Could Help U.S. Customs and Border Protection Improve Border Enforcement Efforts*, GAO-07-735 (Washington, D.C.: Apr. 26, 2007).

[29] If a rule detects a potential threat based on the data for a shipment, the weighted value for that rule contributes to the calculation for the shipment's risk score. If a rule does not detect a potential threat in the data, the rule does not contribute any points to the risk score.

[30] Although it is possible to get a waiver to exempt a high-risk shipment from examination based on information collected, CBP policy states that such waivers should be used judiciously and only when based upon articulable reasons.

[31] In DHS's *Annual Performance Report* for fiscal years 2008 through 2010, DHS reported that CBP did not meet its target for the percentage of maritime cargo containers scanned for contraband in fiscal year 2008. DHS reported that one of the reasons for not meeting the target was that updates to ATS targeting rules resulted in fewer mandatory examinations based on ATS's assessment of a shipment as high risk, and that CBP did not compensate for this decrease by increasing the number of discretionary (CBP officer targeted) exams. DHS reported that CBP planned to increase the number of discretionary exams. According to a CBP official responsible for tracking this information, CBP exceeded its target in fiscal years 2009 through 2011. For example, in fiscal year 2011, CBP scanned 4.13 percent of maritime cargo containers, which exceeded CBP's goal of 3.80 percent. The containers scanned included those that were targeted based on their risk score or other risk factors identified by targeters, as well as for other reasons. For example, CBP officials at all six ATUs we visited said that their ports examine some containers regardless of the risk assessed by ATS or a targeter (e.g., scan every seventh container being unloaded from a

vessel). CBP also has a Compliance Measurement Program that supplements ATS by randomly selecting shipments to be inspected to determine whether the shipments comply with supply chain security and trade laws.

[32] Because the report we issued in August 2006 regarding CBP's targeting practices contains sensitive information, it is not publicly available.

[33] An external peer review is a process that includes an assessment of the model by independent and qualified external experts.

[34] In 2006, CBP referred to its two performance measures as the estimated accuracy rate and the estimated inspection rate, respectively. In more recent assessments, it refers to these measures as the true positive rate and the false positive rate, respectively. In 2006, CBP also calculated the relative performance factor, which provides an assessment of how much better or worse ATS performs at targeting oceangoing cargo shipped in containers than a random selection method.

[35] To determine which shipments to use for the calculations, the consulting firm developed a proxy positive definition of shipments that contain indications of materials or behaviors that are believed to be similar in physical attributes, magnitude, and intent to the materials and behavior of shipments associated with terrorist threats. The firm had to develop this definition because CBP inspections of cargo shipped in containers at that time had not resulted in the identification of any direct terrorism threats. Because CBP had not identified any terrorist-related materials in shipments at the time this report was written, there was no way to validate the proxy positive shipments.

[36] DHS Office of Inspector General, *Cargo Targeting and Examinations*, OIG-10-34 (Washington, D.C.: Jan. 6, 2010).

[37] We compared the results of assessments for the previous version of the weight set with the results of assessments for the current version of the weight set. For the previous version of the weight set, the TPR was about 20 percent from the end of fiscal year 2009 through fiscal year 2010, whereas the TPR for the current weight set has generally been below 10 percent from the third quarter of fiscal year 2011 through the third quarter of fiscal year 2012. According to CBP officials, the measures for each quarter are calculated using data from the prior 1-year period. However, according to CBP officials, the methodologies used to assess each weight set were different, and because it is not clear to what extent this change in methodology accounts for any changes in the performance measures, it is not possible to make a meaningful comparison between the results.

[38] In the past, CBP's decision to update the performance of the weight set was dependent upon feedback from targeters or external reasons—such as the receipt of new data because of the 10+2 rule. However, feedback from targeters is not systematic and may not provide a reliable assessment of the weight set's ability to identify high-risk containers. CBP utilizes ATU targeters at rules conferences to assist in rule and weight set updates because they use ATS for daily operations. CBP receives weight set input from ATU targeters from a variety of ports nationally. CBP headquarters officials consider all input and determine the best way to use the information to indicate risk. In some cases, changes are made to rules that will affect targeting nationwide, whereas in other cases, rule changes may not be implemented because they might have a negative effect across all ports. Further, in some cases, rules that affect only a single port or region may be added to a weight set. According to CBP officials, they do not rely on a particular amount of input to initiate the process of updating the weight set; rather, they subjectively determine the point at which the feedback is substantial enough to warrant an evaluation of the weight set.

End Notes for Appendix II

[1] GAO, *Supply Chain Security: CBP Has Made Progress in Assisting the Trade Industry in Implementing the New Importer Security Filing Requirements, but Some Challenges Remain*, GAO-10-841 (Washington, D.C.: Sept. 10, 2010). Because the reports we issued in February 2004 and August 2006 regarding CBP's targeting practices contain sensitive information, they are not publicly available.

[2] Pub. L. No. 108-293, § 809(g), 118 Stat. 1028, 1087.

[3] Some recommendations from these products addressed other elements of CBP's cargo container security strategy, such as policies and procedures for examining cargo containers. The scope of our review focused on ATS and CBP's targeting efforts, and therefore the recommendations listed in this appendix are those that fall within that scope.

[4] In November 2006, the DHS OIG also reported CBP was in the process of developing national ATS performance measures in response to our February 2004 recommendations. The DHS OIG did not issue any related recommendations in that report. That DHS OIG report contains sensitive information and is therefore not publicly available.

[5] DHS OIG, *Cargo Targeting and Examinations*, OIG-10-34.

[6] DHS OIG, *Audit of Targeting Oceangoing Cargo Containers (Unclassified Summary)*, OIG-05-26.

[7] GAO-10-841.

[8] The DHS OIG report issued in November 2006 contains sensitive information and is therefore not publicly available.

[9] The system discussed in the November 2006 DHS OIG report is the predecessor to the third-party database of public and proprietary records that is mentioned in this report as a tool that targeters use outside of ATS to research supply chain parties involved in a shipment and to inform their decision whether to target a shipment for examination.

In: Supply Chain Security
Editor: Marten Laurits

ISBN: 978-1-62808-230-2

Chapter 2

IT SUPPLY CHAIN: NATIONAL SECURITY - RELATED AGENCIES NEED TO BETTER ADDRESS RISKS*

United States Government Accountability Office

WHY GAO DID THIS STUDY

Federal agencies rely extensively on computerized information systems and electronic data to carry out their operations. The exploitation of information technology (IT) products and services through the global supply chain is an emerging threat that could degrade the confidentiality, integrity, and availability of critical and sensitive agency networks and data.

GAO was asked to identify (1) the key risks associated with the IT supply chains used by federal agencies; (2) the extent to which selected national security-related departments have addressed such risks; and (3) the extent to which those departments have determined that their telecommunication networks contain foreign-developed equipment, software, or services. To do this, GAO analyzed federal acquisition and information security laws, regulations, standards, and guidelines; examined departmental policies and procedures; and interviewed officials from four national security-related departments, the intelligence community, and nonfederal entities.

---

* This is an edited, reformatted and augmented version of United States Government Accountability Office, Publication No. GAO-12-361, dated March 2012.

WHAT GAO RECOMMENDS

GAO is recommending that the Departments of Energy, Homeland Security, and Justice take steps, as needed, to develop and document policies, procedures, and monitoring capabilities that address IT supply chain risk. These departments generally concurred with GAO's recommendations.

WHAT GAO FOUND

Reliance on a global supply chain introduces multiple risks to federal information systems. These risks include threats posed by actors—such as foreign intelligence services or counterfeiters—who may exploit vulnerabilities in the supply chain and thus compromise the confidentiality, integrity, or availability of an end system and the information it contains. This in turn can adversely affect an agency's ability to effectively carry out its mission. Each of the key threats presented in the table below could create an unacceptable risk to federal agencies.

Threats to the IT Supply Chain

Threats
Installation of malicious logic on hardware or software
Installation of counterfeit hardware or software
Failure or disruption in the production or distribution of a critical product or service
Reliance upon a malicious or unqualified service-provider for the performance of technical services
Installation of unintentional vulnerabilities on hardware or software

Source: GAO analysis of unclassified governmental and nongovernmental data.

Although four national security-related departments—the Departments of Energy, Homeland Security, Justice, and Defense—have acknowledged these threats, two of the departments—Energy and Homeland Security—have not yet defined supply chain protection measures for department information systems and are not in a position to have implementing procedures or monitoring capabilities to verify compliance with and effectiveness of any such measures. Justice has identified supply chain protection measures, but has not developed procedures for implementing or monitoring compliance with and effectiveness of these measures. Until comprehensive policies, procedures, and monitoring capabilities are developed, documented, and implemented, it is more likely that these national security-related departments will rely on security measures that are inadequate, ineffective, or inefficient to manage emergent information technology supply chain risks. In contrast, Defense has made greater progress through its incremental approach to supply chain risk management. The department has defined supply chain protection measures and procedures for implementing and monitoring these measures. The four national security-related departments also participate in governmentwide efforts to address supply chain security, including the development of technical and policy tools and collaboration with the intelligence community.

Officials at the four departments stated that their respective agencies have not determined or tracked the extent to which their telecommunications networks contain foreign-developed equipment, software, or services. Federal agencies are not required to track this information, and officials from four components of the U.S. national security community believe that doing so would provide minimal security value relative to cost.

ABBREVIATIONS

CISO	chief information security officer
CNCI	Comprehensive National Cybersecurity Initiative
DHS	Department of Homeland Security
FBI	Federal Bureau of Investigation
FIPS	Federal Information Processing Standards
FISMA	Federal Information Security Management Act
IT	information technology
NIST	National Institute of Standards and Technology
OMB	Office of Management and Budget
SEI	Software Engineering Institute
SP	special publication
US-CERT	U.S. Computer Emergency Readiness Team

March 23, 2012

Congressional Requesters

Information systems, as well as the products and services that support their function, are essential for government operations. Federal agencies rely extensively on computerized information systems and electronic data to carry out their operations. The security of these systems and data is essential to protecting national and economic security.

The exploitation of information technology (IT) products and services through the supply chain is an emerging threat.[1] In January 2012, the Director of National Intelligence identified the vulnerabilities associated with the IT supply chain for the nation's networks as one of the greatest strategic cyber threat challenges the country faces.[2] IT supply chain-related threats can be introduced in the manufacturing, assembly, and distribution of hardware, software, and services. Moreover, these threats can appear at each phase of the system development life cycle, when an agency initiates, develops, implements, maintains, and disposes of an information system. As a result, the compromise of an agency's IT supply chain can degrade the confidentiality, integrity, and availability of its critical and sensitive networks, IT-enabled equipment, and data.

Safeguarding federal computer systems is a continuing challenge. We have consistently identified significant weaknesses in the security controls for federal systems and networks and in the associated agencies' information security programs that have jeopardized the confidentiality, integrity, and availability of government information. Because of the persistent nature of these vulnerabilities and associated risks, we have designated information security as a governmentwide high-risk issue since 1997 in our biennial reports to Congress.[3] In addition, challenges associated with the acquisition of information systems have contributed to other high-risk designations. For example, we have identified the Department of Defense (Defense) business systems modernization and the implementation and transformation of the Department of Homeland Security (DHS) as high-risk issues, which include challenges associated with their respective systems acquisitions.[4]

Our objectives were to identify (1) the key risks associated with the supply chains used by federal agencies to procure IT equipment, software, or services;[5] (2) the extent to which selected national security-related agencies have addressed IT supply chain risks; and (3) the extent to which national security-related federal agencies have determined that their telecommunications networks contain foreign-developed equipment, software, or services. To identify key risks, we analyzed government and nongovernment reports on IT supply chain risks. We also validated identified threats with experts from the Office of the Director of National Intelligence, the National Security Agency, the Central Intelligence Agency, and the Defense Intelligence Agency. To identify department efforts to address IT supply chain risks, we analyzed department information security policies and procedures and interviewed senior information security program officials at the Department of Energy (Energy), the Department of Justice (Justice), DHS, and Defense. These departments were selected because of their national security-related duties. To identify the extent to which the departments have identified foreign-developed equipment, software, and services, we analyzed federal statutes, regulations, and policies to determine whether any tracking requirements exist. We also interviewed agency officials regarding their current efforts to determine and track country-of-origin information for their IT equipment, software, and services. Further, we interviewed federal officials from four components of the national security community to identify potential costs and benefits associated with tracking the country of origin of IT equipment, software, or services. Additional details of our objectives, scope, and methodology are included in appendix I.

We conducted this performance audit from November 2010 to March 2012 in accordance with generally accepted government auditing standards. Those standards require that we plan and perform the audit to obtain sufficient, appropriate evidence to provide a reasonable basis for our findings and conclusions based on our audit objectives. We believe that the evidence obtained provides a reasonable basis for our findings and conclusions based on our audit objectives.

BACKGROUND

Information systems can be complex undertakings consisting of a multitude of pieces of equipment, software products, and service providers. Each of these components may rely on one or more supply chains. Obtaining a full understanding of the sources of a given information system during initiation and development can also be extremely complex. According to the Software Engineering Institute (SEI), the identity of each product or service provider may not be visible to others in the supply chain.[6] Typically, an acquirer (such as a federal agency) will only know about the participants directly connected to it in the supply chain. As a result, an acquirer will have little visibility into the supply chains of its suppliers.[7] For example, a program office at a federal agency may rely on a prime contractor to acquire, develop, and maintain an information system. In turn, the prime contractor may obtain the equipment, software, and services that constitute the system through various means, including the

- reuse of existing equipment or legacy software;
- outsourcing of system development to an additional supplier;
- development of the capability in-house; or
- acquisition of the capability directly from a supplier or commercial offthe-shelf-vendor, or through open-source means.

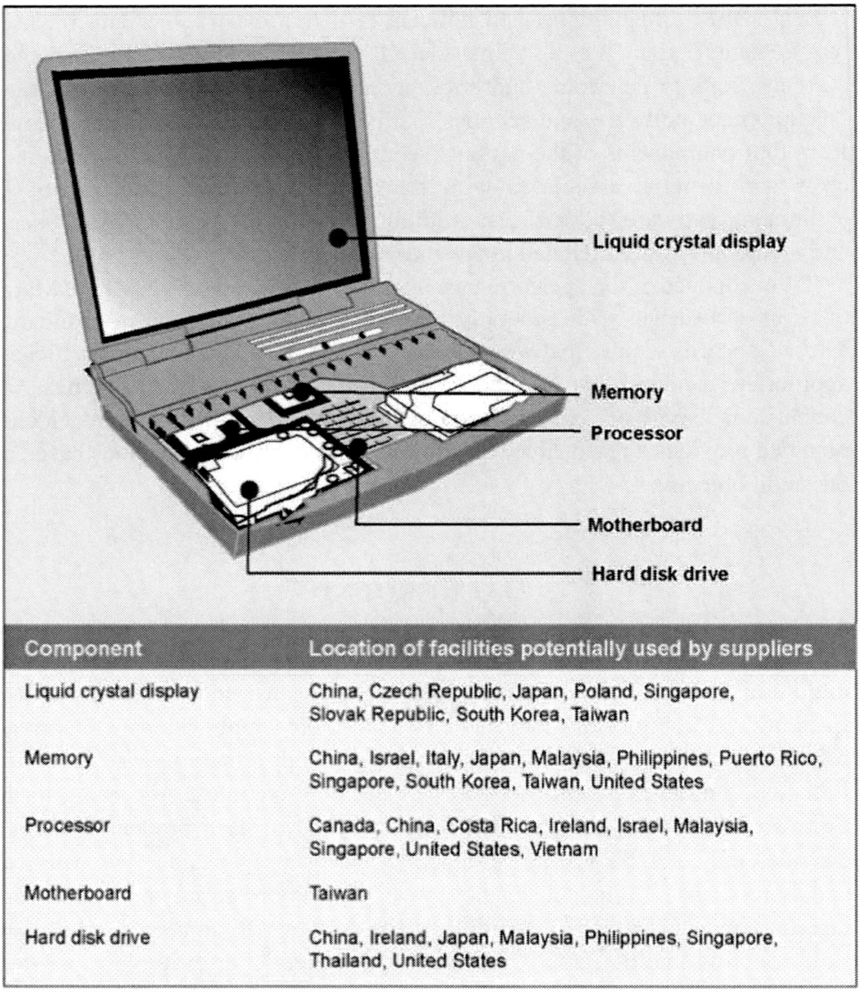

Component	Location of facilities potentially used by suppliers
Liquid crystal display	China, Czech Republic, Japan, Poland, Singapore, Slovak Republic, South Korea, Taiwan
Memory	China, Israel, Italy, Japan, Malaysia, Philippines, Puerto Rico, Singapore, South Korea, Taiwan, United States
Processor	Canada, China, Costa Rica, Ireland, Israel, Malaysia, Singapore, United States, Vietnam
Motherboard	Taiwan
Hard disk drive	China, Ireland, Japan, Malaysia, Philippines, Singapore, Thailand, United States

Source: GAO analysis of public information.

Figure 1. Potential Origins of Common Suppliers for Laptop Components.

In addition, the complexity of corporate structures, in which a parent company (or its subsidiaries) may own or control IT companies that conduct business under different names in multiple countries, presents additional challenges to obtaining a full understanding of the source of an information system. According to NIST, today's complex global economy and manufacturing practices make corporate ownership and control more ambiguous when assessing supply chain vulnerabilities. For example, foreign-based companies sometimes manufacture and assemble products and components in the United States, and U.S.-based companies sometimes manufacture products and components overseas, or domestically employ foreign workers.

Commercial providers of IT use a global supply chain to design, develop, manufacture, and distribute hardware and software products throughout the world. Many of the manufacturing inputs required for those products—whether physical materials or knowledge—are acquired from various sources around the globe. Figure 1 depicts the potential countries of origin of the common suppliers for various components within a commercially available computer.

Federal Policy Promotes the Use of Commercial IT

Federal procurement law and policies promote the acquisition of commercial products when they meet the government's needs. For example, provisions of the Federal Acquisition Streamlining Act of 1994 are designed to encourage the government to buy commercial items by (1) requiring a preference for commercial items where feasible, and (2) making exceptions to certain government requirements that previously discouraged commercial vendors from offering their products and services to the government. In addition, Office of Management and Budget (OMB) Circular A-130 requires that agencies select investments in information technology (such as computers, software, firmware,[8] and support services) that, among other things, make maximum use of commercial, off-the-shelf technology.[9] OMB Circular A-130 also requires that agencies acquire off-the-shelf software from commercial sources unless developing custom software has been documented as more cost-effective.

The Comprehensive National Cybersecurity Initiative Recognizes Supply Chain Risk to Federal IT

In 2008, the Bush administration began to implement a series of initiatives, referred to as the Comprehensive National Cybersecurity Initiative (CNCI), aimed primarily at improving cybersecurity within the federal government. Specifically, CNCI is composed of a set of 12 initiatives with the objective of safeguarding federal executive branch information systems by reducing potential vulnerabilities; protecting against intrusion attempts; and anticipating future threats through defensive, offensive, educational, research and development, and counterintelligence efforts.

One of the CNCI initiatives focused on developing a multipronged approach for addressing global supply chain risk management. Specifically, the initiative stated that risks stemming from both the domestic and global supply chains must be managed in a strategic and comprehensive way over the entire life cycle of products, systems, and services. It further states that managing this risk will require

- a greater awareness of the threats, vulnerabilities, and consequences associated with acquisition decisions;
- the development and employment of tools and resources to technically and operationally mitigate risk across the life cycle of products (from design through retirement);
- the development of new acquisition policies and practices that reflect the complex global marketplace; and
- partnership with industry to develop and adopt supply chain risk management standards and best practices.

In March 2010, we reported on the actions that had been taken to develop interagency mechanisms to plan and coordinate CNCI activities and the challenges the CNCI faced in achieving its objectives related to securing federal information systems.[10] We determined that the White House and federal agencies had taken steps to plan and coordinate CNCI activities by establishing several interagency work groups. We also determined that the CNCI faced several challenges in meeting its objectives, including defining roles and responsibilities, establishing measures of effectiveness, and establishing an appropriate level of transparency (including for supply chain risk management activities). We made six recommendations to OMB to address the identified challenges. OMB concurred with five of our six recommendations and has since taken steps to address most of these challenges, including clarifying cybersecurity responsibilities and activities among federal entities.

Federal Law Requires Agencies to Establish Information Security Programs, and Implementing Standards and Guidelines Provide for Management of Supply Chain-Related Risk

The Federal Information Security Management Act of 2002 (FISMA) establishes federal agency information security program requirements that support the effectiveness of information security controls over information resources that support federal operations and assets.[11] Its framework creates a cycle of risk management activities necessary for an effective security program. FISMA requires every federal agency to establish an information security program. Additionally, the act assigns responsibility to NIST to provide standards and guidelines to agencies on information security.[12]

FISMA directed NIST to promulgate federal standards for (1) the security categorization of federal information and information systems based on the objective of providing appropriate levels of information security according to a range of risk levels, and (2) minimum security requirements for information and information systems in each such category. NIST subsequently issued two Federal Information Processing Standards (FIPS):

- FIPS 199 is to be used to categorize information and information systems, thereby providing a common framework for expressing security.[13] Under this standard, a system is categorized (high, moderate, or low[14]) based on the type of impact that would result from a loss of confidentiality, integrity, or availability.
- FIPS 200 addresses the specification of minimum security requirements for federal information and information systems. [15] In particular, FIPS 200 directs federal agencies to meet the minimum security requirements through the use of the security controls in accordance with NIST Special Publication 800-53 (SP 800-53).[16]

NIST issued SP 800-53 to provide a catalog of security controls and technical guidelines that federal agencies use to protect federal information and information systems. After conducting the security categorization process established by FIPS 199, organizations are required to select an appropriately tailored set of initial security controls consistent with the baselines in SP 800-53. In August 2009, NIST published SP 800-53, Revision 3, which, for the first time, included a security control for supply chain protection (SA-12).[17] As part of SA-12, NIST identified several specific measures that organizations could use to provide additional supply chain protections. These include, but are not limited to,

- conducting a due diligence review of suppliers prior to entering into contractual agreements to acquire information system hardware, software, firmware, or services;
- using trusted shipping and warehousing for information systems, information system components, and information technology products; and
- employing independent analysis and penetration testing against delivered information systems, information system components, and information technology products.[18]

SP 800-53, Revision 3, also includes a security control for system and services acquisition policy and procedures (SA-1).[19] Thus, for systems where both controls are selected, agencies should develop, disseminate, and review acquisition policy and implementing procedures that help protect against supply chain threats throughout the system development life cycle.

Other policy requires SP 800-53 controls to be selected for both non-national security and national security systems. Specifically, OMB Circular A-130 states that federal agencies are required to use SP 800-53 in selecting and specifying controls for non-national security programs. Also, in October 2009, the Committee on National Security Systems published Instruction 1253, 20 which establishes SP 800-53 as a common foundation for information security controls for national security systems.[21] Under this instruction, all national security systems are directed to select SA-1 as part of their initial control baselines. Further, all national security systems that are categorized as high or moderate impact for integrity are directed to select SA-12 as part of their initial control baselines.[22]

In March 2011, NIST published SP 800-39, which provides an approach for organizationwide management of information security risk, including those related to supply chains.[23] Among other things, the publication states that risk management requires organizations to monitor risk on an ongoing basis as part of a comprehensive risk management program. Monitoring programs can aid agency officials in oversight of currently implemented security controls. To support risk monitoring, organizations are expected to describe how compliance with security requirements is verified and how the organization will determine the effectiveness of risk response activities.

In addition, the Ike Skelton National Defense Authorization Act for Fiscal Year 2011 included provisions related to supply chain security. Specifically, Section 806 authorizes the Secretaries of Defense, the Army, the Navy, and the Air Force to exclude a contractor from specified types of procurements on the basis of a determination of significant supply chain risk to a covered system. 24 Section 806 also establishes requirements for limiting disclosure of the basis of such procurement action.

NIST Plans to Issue Further Guidance on IT Supply Chain Practices

In June 2010, NIST released a draft interagency report, *Piloting Supply Chain Risk Management Practices for Federal Information Systems,*[25] which, when finalized and published, is intended to provide agencies with supply chain risk mitigation strategies integrated with the information systems development life cycle. Its methodology for handling supply chain risk included, among other things, determining which procurements should consider supply chain risk, working with agency stakeholders to help mitigate supply chain risk, and describing roles and responsibilities within the agency. NIST plans to release the final version of the report by the end of fiscal year 2012. In February 2012, NIST released for comment the initial public draft of SP 800-53, Revision 4, which, when finalized and published, is intended to provide, among other things, additional supply chain-related guidance and protection measures.[26] The draft revised SA-12 guidance and incorporated supply chain considerations into, among other things, security measures related to incident handling and reporting. NIST anticipates the publication of the final document in July 2012.

IT Supply Chain Presents Numerous Information Security Risks to Federal Agencies

Reliance on a global supply chain introduces multiple risks to federal information systems and underscores the importance of threat assessments and risk mitigation. These risks include threats posed by actors—such as foreign intelligence services or counterfeiters—who may exploit vulnerabilities in the supply chain, thus compromising the confidentiality, integrity, or availability of the end-system and the information it contains.[27] This in turn can adversely affect an agency's ability to carry out its mission.

The IT Supply Chain Faces Threats

Supply chain-related threats are present at various phases of the system development life cycle. Each of the key threats presented in table 1 could create an unacceptable risk to federal agencies.

Table 1. Threats to the IT Supply Chain

- Installation of hardware or software containing malicious logic
- Installation of counterfeit hardware or software
- Failure or disruption in the production or distribution of critical products
- Reliance on a malicious or unqualified service provider for the performance of technical services
- Installation of hardware or software that contains unintentional vulnerabilities

Source: GAO analysis of unclassified governmental and nongovernmental data.

Installation of Hardware or Software Containing Malicious Logic

Threat actors can use the supply chain to insert hardware or software containing malicious logic through tampering during the development and implementation of an information system. Malicious logic is hardware, firmware, or software that is intentionally included or inserted in a system for a harmful purpose. For example, viruses and Trojan horses are two forms of malicious logic that could be included in a system via the supply chain. A virus is a computer program that can copy itself and infect a computer without permission or knowledge of the user. A Trojan horse is a computer program that appears to have a useful function, but also has a hidden and potentially malicious function that evades security mechanisms, sometimes by exploiting legitimate authorizations of a system entity that invokes the program.

Malicious logic can cause significant damage by allowing attackers to take control of entire systems and thereby read, modify, or delete sensitive information; disrupt operations; launch attacks against other organizations' systems; or destroy systems.[28] For example, it was reported in 2008 that hardware similar to flash memory drives that was released by a major U.S. electronics manufacturer contained malicious code that could allow an attacker to take over an infected system.[29] Additionally, recent information reported by DHS indicates that malicious code attacks are prevalent in the federal environment. Specifically, according to the United States Computer Emergency Readiness Team (US-CERT), approximately 27 percent of the 42,854 agency-reported security incidents during fiscal year 2011 involved malicious code.[30] Although not necessarily the result of an IT supply chain attack, these incidents highlight the impact that such attacks could have on agency operations.

Installation of Counterfeit Hardware or Software

Counterfeit information technology is hardware or software that contains nongenuine component parts or code. A component is not genuine if it (1) is an unauthorized copy; (2) does not conform to the design, model, or performance standards as prescribed by the original component manufacturer; (3) is not produced by the original component manufacturer or is produced by an unauthorized contractor; (4) is an off-specification, defective, or used original component manufacturer product sold as "new" or working; or (5) has incorrect or false markings or documentation.

The Defense Department's Information Assurance Technology Analysis Center has reported that counterfeit information technology threatens the integrity, trustworthiness, and reliability of information systems for several reasons, including the facts that (1) counterfeits are usually less reliable and therefore fail more often and more quickly than genuine parts, and (2) counterfeiting presents an opportunity for the counterfeiter to insert malicious logic or backdoors[31] into the replicas or copies that would be far more difficult in more secure manufacturing facilities.[32] Federal agencies have unintentionally purchased counterfeit IT products. For example, according to a Cisco report about the counterfeiting of its products, one case involved the illegal modification of routers with fake seals and Cisco tape to appear as if they contained security protections of a model valued at twice as much as a standard version. These routers were then purchased by a reseller and sold to the federal government through an official government solicitation for purchase. Additionally, according to the United States Attorney's Office for the Southern District of Texas, the Marine Corps, Air Force, Federal Aviation Administration, and Federal Bureau of Investigation (FBI) allegedly purchased counterfeit Cisco products that had originated in China.[33] As a result, these agencies were at increased risk of installing products that were less reliable or secure than authentic IT equipment.

Failure or Disruption in the Production or Distribution of Critical Products

Failure or disruption in the production or distribution of a critical product could affect the availability of information technology equipment that is used to support federal information systems. Both man-made (e.g., disruptions caused by labor or political disputes) and natural causes (e.g., earthquakes, fires, floods, or hurricanes) could disrupt the supply of IT products critical to the operations of federal agencies. For example, following a severe Japanese earthquake in March 2011, it was reported that damage to Japan's semiconductor industry could affect the availability of computer memory on the global market, because approximately 40 percent of certain types of computer memory is manufactured in Japan. [34] In addition, according to the U.S.-China Economic and Security Commission, rare earth elements are a collection of 17 elements that are critical to commercial and military high-technology applications.[35] These elements are distributed globally, with China reportedly producing approximately 97 percent of the current world supply. As a result, a disruption in the supply chain for rare earth elements could reduce the availability of material necessary for the U.S. government to develop systems.

Reliance on a Malicious or Unqualified Service Provider for the Performance of Technical Services

Contractors and other service providers may, by virtue of their position, have access to federal data and systems. As we have previously reported, service providers could attempt to use their access to obtain sensitive information, commit fraud, disrupt operations, or launch attacks against other computer systems and networks.[36] We have also reported that the FBI has identified multiple sources of threats, such as foreign entities engaged in intelligence gathering and information warfare, criminals, and disgruntled employees or contractors working within an organization.[37] As an example of this type of threat, according to a United States Attorney's Office press release, a contract programmer was charged with stealing software code from the Federal Reserve Bank of New York.[38] Further, an FBI official alleged that this individual took advantage of the access associated with his position in order to steal highly sensitive source code.

Table 2. Examples of Supply Chain Vulnerabilities

Vulnerability	Description	Threat example
Acquisition of information technology products or parts from independent distributors, brokers, or the gray market	Purchasing from a source other than an original component manufacturer or authorized reseller may increase an agency's risk of encountering substandard, subverted, and counterfeit products. Independent distributors purchase new parts with the intention to sell and redistribute them back into the market, without having a contractual agreement with the original component manufacturer. Brokers are a type of independent distributor that work in a just-in-time inventory environment and search the industry and locate parts for customers as requested. The gray market refers to the trade of parts through distribution channels that, while legal, are unofficial, unauthorized, or unintended by the original component manufacturer.	Installation of counterfeit hardware orsoftware
Lack of adequate testing for software updates and patches	Applying untested updates and patches to information system components may increase an agency's risk that an attacker could insert malicious code of its choosing into a system. For example, if an agency or contractor fails to validate the authenticity of patches with suppliers, an attacker could write a fake patch that might allow unauthorized access to information in the system.	Installation of hardware or software containing malicious logic
Incomplete information on IT suppliers	Acquiring IT equipment, software, or services from suppliers without understanding the supplier's past performance or corporate structure may increase the risk of (1) encountering substandard, subverted, and counterfeit products, or (2) providing adversaries of the United States with access to sensitive agency systems or information. For example, lacking information concerning an IT service provider's corporate structure could reduce an agency's ability to assess whether or not the service provider or its employees are subject to undue foreign control or influence.	Installation of hardware or software containing malicious logic Installation of hardware or software that contains unintentional vulnerabilities Installation of counterfeit hardware or software Failure or disruption in the production ordistribution of critical products Reliance on a malicious or unqualified service provider for the performance of technical services

Table 2. (Continued)

Vulnerability	Description	Threat example
Use of supply chain delivery and storage mechanisms that are not secure	Using delivery or storage mechanisms that are not secure may increase the risk that an IT product is intercepted or subverted while it is in transit to the agency or while it is in storage before installation. This vulnerability may allow a threat actor to gain unauthorized access to the IT product, thereby facilitating unauthorized modification, substitution, or diversion. Unsecured delivery and storage mechanisms may also lead to the exposure of sensitive information to unauthorized parties, such as the identity of the agency purchasing the IT product or how the IT product will be used.	Installation of hardware or software containing malicious logic Failure or disruption in the production ordistribution of critical products Installation of counterfeit hardware or software

Source: GAO analysis of unclassified governmental and nongovernmental data.

Installation of Hardware or Software That Contains Unintentional Vulnerabilities

Unintentional vulnerabilities are hardware, software, or firmware that are included or inserted in a system and that inadvertently present opportunities for compromise. It has been reported that attackers focus their efforts on, among other things, finding and exploiting existing defects—such as buffer overflows—in the code, which are usually the result of unintentional coding errors.[39]

For example, DHS recently released an alert that identified vulnerabilities in certain firmware used by industrial control systems.[40] The vulnerabilities identified could allow remote attackers to, among other things, cause a denial of service.[41]

Vulnerabilities in Acquisition or Information Security Controls Are Exploitable

The threats described above can pose risk to federal information systems. Specifically, threat actors can introduce the above-mentioned threats by exploiting vulnerabilities that could exist at multiple points in the global supply chain.

In addition, supply chain vulnerabilities can include weaknesses in agency acquisition or information security procedures, controls, or implementation related to a federal information system. If a threat actor exploits an existing vulnerability, it could lead to the loss of confidentiality, integrity, or availability of the end-system and associated information. Table 2 describes examples of the types of vulnerabilities that could be exploited.

THREE NATIONAL SECURITY-RELATED AGENCIES HAVE NOT FULLY ADDRESSED IT SUPPLY CHAIN RISK

Although the four agencies in our review have acknowledged the risks presented by supply chain vulnerabilities, two of the agencies—Energy and DHS—have not yet defined supply chain protection measures for department information systems and are not in a position to have implementing procedures or monitoring capabilities to verify compliance with and effectiveness of any such measures.

Justice has identified supply chain protection measures, but has not developed procedures for implementing or monitoring compliance with and the effectiveness of these measures. In contrast, Defense has made greater progress through its incremental approach to supply chain risk management. Specifically, it has defined supply chain protection measures and implementing procedures, and plans to develop outcome-based performance measures as the agency's supply chain risk management capabilities mature.

According to the NIST SP 800-53 control for supply chain protection, agencies should define which security measures, if any, should be employed to protect against supply chain threats. In addition, the NIST SP 800-53 control for system and service acquisition calls for agencies to develop, document, and disseminate procedures to ensure the effective implementation of these measures.

These procedures can be developed for the agency's security program in general, or for a particular information system when required. Finally, according to NIST SP 800-39, agencies should also implement monitoring mechanisms to verify compliance with, and determine the effectiveness of, established security controls and associated supply chain protection measures.

Energy Lacks IT Supply Chain Measures, Documented Procedures, and Monitoring Capabilities

Energy has not defined security measures that information system owners should employ to protect against supply chain threats. In May 2011, the department revised its information security program, which sets forth requirements and responsibilities to protect departmental information and information systems. The program document requires Energy components to implement its provisions based on requirements and guidance defined by NIST and the Committee on National Security Systems, which includes the IT supply chain protection control. According to Energy's chief information security officer (CISO), the department is in the process of implementing the program, and a large percentage of the department will be covered by the end of fiscal year 2012. However, the department was unable to provide details on implementation progress, milestones for completion, or how supply chain protection measures would be defined.

Additionally, without defined supply chain security measures, Energy is not in a position to develop, document, and disseminate procedures to ensure the effective implementation of supply chain protection. The development of implementation procedures relies on the department defining its supply chain security measures.

Further, Energy is not in a position to implement a monitoring capability to verify compliance with, and determine the effectiveness of, any such protections. The department's information security program does describe high-level efforts to monitor risks to Energy information systems.

However, it does not specify any monitoring or compliance efforts related to IT supply chain measures because Energy has not yet defined what supply chain measures will be employed by system owners.

Until Energy ensures that IT supply chain protection measures and implementing procedures are developed, documented, and disseminated, officials will be without essential guidance that facilitates the effective and consistent implementation of supply chain protection on departmental information systems. Further, senior Energy leadership will not have an effective monitoring capability to provide them with the information necessary to make informed decisions on supply chain protection activities. Implementing a monitoring capability for any supply chain security measures can help ensure that measures are adequate in the face of changes in threats, departmental operations, or level of compliance.

DHS Lacks IT Supply Chain Measures, Documented Procedures, and Monitoring Capabilities

Although its information security guidance mentions the SP 800-53 control related to supply chain protection, DHS has not defined the measures that system owners should employ. Under DHS's information security program, the department's CISO is responsible for issuing departmentwide information security policy that incorporates NIST guidelines and applicable OMB memorandums and circulars for all DHS systems and networks. The department's information security policy manager stated that DHS had not addressed IT supply chain security through its policy. The official stated that DHS is currently in the process of developing such policy, but provided no details on when it would be completed.

Additionally, in the absence of defined supply chain security measures, DHS is not in a position to develop, document, or disseminate procedures to ensure the effective implementation of supply chain protection. DHS issued a handbook to provide specific techniques and procedures for implementing the department's information security policy; however, it does not include any supply chain-related implementation guidance. This is due to the fact that the department has not yet defined what supply chain measures will be employed by system owners.

The department also is not in a position to implement a monitoring mechanism to assess the compliance with and effectiveness of IT supply chain security measures. DHS's information security policy does describe high-level monitoring for compliance and effectiveness of its information security program, including its components performing assessments against the controls identified in NIST SP 800-53. However, the policy does not specify any monitoring or compliance efforts related to IT supply chain measures, because the department has not yet defined what supply chain measures will be employed by system owners.

Until DHS updates its information security policy to ensure that IT supply chain protection measures and implementing procedures are developed and documented, officials will be without essential guidance that is required to effectively implement supply chain protection on departmental information systems. Further, senior DHS leadership will not have an effective monitoring capability that provides the information that is necessary to make informed decisions on supply chain protection activities. Implementing a monitoring capability for any supply chain security measures can help ensure that measures are adequate in the face of changes in threats, departmental operations, or level of compliance.

Justice Has Defined Supply Chain Measures, but Lacks Documented Procedures and Monitoring Capabilities

Justice has defined specific security measures that information system owners should employ to protect against supply chain threats. The department's minimum security control requirements specify that supply chain protection for high-impact systems is to be provided through the use of vendor acquisition contracts and agreements. In particular, Justice officials identified two generic contract provisions that could be used to address supply chain threats: (1) a citizenship and residency requirement and (2) a national security risk questionnaire (including a Foreign Ownership Control and Influence review).

However, Justice has not developed, documented, and disseminated procedures to ensure the effective implementation of these supply chain protection measures. Specifically, Justice officials were not able to identify which acquisitions would need to have the provisions inserted. Although the Justice CISO stated that the agency would require a national security risk questionnaire based on a national security and departmental mission impact determination, Justice officials could not identify documented criteria that would help security officers and other officials make this determination.

Further, Justice has not implemented a monitoring mechanism to verify compliance with, and determine the effectiveness of, its supply chain security measures. Justice's CISO stated that the department did not have a system to track the use and effectiveness of the contract provisions across all components. As a result, departmental officials were not able to identify the frequency with which the provisions had been inserted into contracts for IT equipment, software, or services. In addition, Justice officials stated that the results of the Foreign Ownership Control and Influence reviews conducted under the provisions were generally kept with the program offices and acquisitions officials. Justice's CISO stated that one reason for not monitoring is that the department is waiting for CNCI initiative 11 and the Committee on

National Security Systems to produce guidance related to monitoring supply chain risk.

Until the department develops, documents, and disseminates procedures to implement its policy on IT supply chain protection, and implements a process to monitor that policy, Justice officials have limited assurance that departmental information systems are being adequately protected against supply chain threats.

Defense Has Issued, and Monitors Compliance with, Supply Chain Measures and Implementation Procedures

Defense's supply chain risk management efforts began in 2003 and include multiple policies that specify measures to be employed for supply chain protection.[42] For example, in February 2009, the department issued policy that requires that supply chain risk be addressed early and across the entire system life cycle.[43] This policy applies to those systems that handle information that the agency determines is critical—in terms of both content and timeliness—to the readiness or effectiveness of the armed forces. The policy calls for the incremental implementation of supply chain risk management through a series of pilot projects. According to the policy, the target date for achieving full operational capability for supply chain risk management is fiscal year 2016. An official from Trusted Mission Systems and Networks, an office within the Defense Office of the Chief Information Officer, stated that lessons learned from the pilots should aid in the implementation of supply chain protection throughout the system development life cycle in a manner that enables systems to meet departmental cost, schedule, and performance requirements.[44]

In addition, the 2009 policy states that the supply chain pilots shall include, among other things,

- processes to assess threats from potential suppliers providing critical components to applicable systems;
- processes to detect the occurrence, reduce the likelihood of occurrence, and mitigate the consequences of products containing counterfeit components or malicious functions; and
- enhanced developmental and operational test and evaluation capabilities, including software vulnerability detection methods and automated tools.

In addition, a July 2011 memorandum, which was issued by the Principal Deputy Under Secretary of Defense for Acquisition, Technology, and Logistics, requires every acquisition program to submit and update a "program protection plan" at each milestone of Defense's system acquisition process. Among other things, program protection is intended to be the integrating process for managing risks to advanced technology and mission-critical system functionality from supply chain exploits or design vulnerabilities throughout the acquisition life cycle.

Defense has developed, documented, and disseminated procedures to facilitate the effective incremental implementation of supply chain protection measures. In February 2010, the department released a supply chain risk management *Key Practices and Implementation Guide*, which describes 32 specific measures that an organization could take to enhance supply chain protection. Examples of these measures include

- maximizing visibility into suppliers;
- choosing programming languages, subsets, and tools that counter weaknesses; and
- reducing supply chain risks during software updates and patch management.[45]

Defense has also developed, documented, and disseminated procedures related to program protection plans. According to these procedures, program protection plans should guide a program office's security measures, and should be updated as threats and vulnerabilities change or are better understood. The procedures identify at least four ways in which Defense programs should manage supply chain risk. Specifically, the procedures recommend that program officials

- identify critical program information, critical functions, and components;[46]
- document how supply chain threat assessments will be used to influence system design, development environment, and procurement practices;
- assess the need for trusted suppliers for integrated circuits; and
- identify specific counterfeit protection measures.

Defense has also implemented a monitoring mechanism to determine the status and effectiveness of its supply chain protection pilots. Trusted Mission

Systems and Networks is responsible for collecting supply chain risk management data and metrics on pilot efforts and reporting the results of the pilots conducted between 2009 and 2010. For example, this office issued a limited release report, dated April 2011, that described the findings and lessons learned related to supply chain protection. According to the report, this information was based on data collected from the 2010 supply chain pilots conducted in fiscal years 2009 and 2010. An official within Trusted Mission Systems and Networks stated that the office has continued to provide quarterly reports on the status and lessons learned from ongoing pilot activities.

In addition, Defense has monitored compliance with, and the effectiveness of, program protection policy and procedures for several acquisition programs. According to the Deputy Director for Program Protection, Office of the Under Secretary of Defense for Acquisition, Technology, and Logistics, the office has conducted six milestone reviews since July 2011.[47] We observed evidence that, for four of the milestone reviews, appropriate Defense officials had verified whether or not the acquisition program had complied with the July 2011 memo and procedures related to program protection planning. For example, the documentation associated with one review conditioned approval on program officials completing an analysis to identify critical components and information within 180 days of the milestone review decision. Regarding the two remaining programs, Defense Systems Engineering officials documented deficiencies in the program protection plan for one of the programs, and, according to the Deputy Director for Program Protection, Office of the Under Secretary of Defense for Acquisition, Technology, and Logistics, these deficiencies were communicated to senior officials prior to the milestone review decision. The remaining program was not approved for continued development.

According to Trusted Mission Systems and Networks officials, the department is collecting metrics to assess the effectiveness of the supply chain risk management aspects of protection planning. Specifically, officials stated that the department is currently collecting data concerning the extent to which the department has engaged with program managers to understand supply chain threats, conducted criticality analyses to identify critical functions, and developed appropriate countermeasures and mitigations. According to an official within Trusted Mission Systems and Networks, the department had conducted 63 such engagements during fiscal year 2011.

National Security-Related Agencies Participate in Governmentwide Efforts to Address Supply Chain Security

The four national security-related agencies also participate in interagency efforts to address supply chain security. These include participation in the CNCI, development of technical and policy tools, and collaboration with the intelligence community.

In support of the CNCI, Defense and DHS jointly lead an interagency initiative on supply chain risk management to address issues of globalization affecting the federal government's IT. Defense's pilot program is intended to provide a basis for supply chain risk management policy recommendations to other federal agencies.

In April 2011, Defense reported conducting supply chain risk management pilots and developed findings related to the need for (1) effective staffing and funding of supply chain risk management activities, (2) enterprise governance of supply chain risk management issues and mitigations, (3) processes and procedures to enhance trust and reduce risk in IT, (4) legal and contractual methods—including new legislation—to avoid using those suppliers determined to present elevated supply chain risk, and (5) revised agency policy to address supply chain risk management.

Additionally, DHS has developed a comprehensive portfolio of technical and policy-based product offerings for federal civilian departments and agencies. These services are incorporated into the set of capabilities offered by DHS's National Cyber Security Division's Supply Chain Risk Management Program, including technical assessment capabilities, acquisition support, and incident response capabilities. These services include the following:

- **Technical risk assessments:** A comprehensive set of technical risk assessment capabilities that includes destructive and nondestructive analysis, code review and assessment, development of attack graphs, vulnerability assessments, and mitigation recommendations.
- **Acquisition threat and risk assessments:** Department and agency program managers can submit system acquisition requirements for review and comment and will receive vendor risk assessment reports on vendors competing for the acquisition and potential mitigations for any identified risk.
- **Incident response and supply chain risk management analysis:** The Supply Chain Risk Management Program has been working in cooperation with US-CERT to develop integrated analysis and

response capabilities for supply chain incidents into its existing missions.

- **DHS supply chain risk management product offerings:** Operational activities to support federal civilian department and agency efforts to manage information technology supply chain risk. These include assessment of agencies' supply chain risk management capabilities and support of ongoing or future acquisitions, as well as technical analysis of hardware and software.

Additionally, in March 2012, the Committee on National Security Systems issued a directive that directs agencies with national security systems to implement a supply chain risk management program.[48] The directive lists available best practices, tools, and resources, including those developed under CNCI efforts and Defense's supply chain pilots. According to Defense and DHS officials, departments and agencies from Defense, the intelligence community, and the civilian agencies collaborated in developing this directive.

Further, Energy, DHS, Defense, and a component of Justice–the FBI—have contributed, to varying degrees, to the development of a common methodology for conducting threat assessments on entities that do business with the national security community.

Under this initiative, which is led by the Office of the National Counterintelligence Executive, 49 agencies are requested to provide copies of threat assessments to a centrally maintained database where they are stored for future use by components of the national security community. In addition, officials from Energy, DHS, Defense, and the FBI stated that they have, or have had, agency officials assigned to the office to facilitate threat information sharing. According to National Counterintelligence Executive officials, the four national security-related agencies have contributed 40 percent of the threat assessments available since 2009. Specifically, Energy has contributed 1 percent, DHS has contributed 4 percent, FBI has contributed 9 percent, and Defense or its components have contributed 26 percent of the threat assessments.

Officials further stated that the vast majority of these assessments relate to firms within the IT industry, and the remainder relate to Defense weapons systems.

Agencies Have Not Determined the Extent of Foreign - Developed IT Telecommunications Equipment, Software, or Services

Officials within the offices of the chief information officer at the Departments of Energy, Homeland Security, and Defense, and the Justice Management Division stated that their respective agencies have not determined and do not currently track the extent to which their telecommunications networks contain foreign-developed equipment, software, or services.

Federal law and regulation do not require federal agencies to track the country of origin of the telecommunications equipment, software, and services that they procure. Although a number of federal laws authorize a preference for American supplies or end products, these laws are of limited use for enhancing information assurance. For example, the Buy American Act, which is designed to promote national commerce and industry, generally (1) restricts federal agencies' purchase of nondomestic ("foreign") manufactured products, and (2) requires that each federal agency report to Congress annually for fiscal years 2009-2011 on the amount of acquisitions it made from entities that manufactured end products outside the United States. Under the act, however, an end product can be considered domestic even if it contains foreign components. Moreover, as implemented, the act does not apply to the acquisition of commercial IT products, which means that the government may purchase commercial IT without regard to the Buy American Act and its reporting requirements. Similarly, the Berry Amendment, which requires domestic sourcing by Defense of specialty metals, also has limited value for IT assurance. Specifically, the Berry Amendment does not apply to either electronic components or commercially available offthe-shelf items containing specialty metals.[50]

In addition, federal officials from four components of the national security community provided reasons why the cost of tracking IT equipment's country of origin outweighs the potential benefits. First, officials from the Director of National Intelligence and the National Security Agency stated that the relationship between a company and a foreign military or intelligence service is a more reliable indicator of a potential security risk than whether a product was manufactured outside the United States. Second, officials from the Director of National Intelligence, Defense Intelligence Agency, and the National Security Agency stated that tracking the country of origin alone would not be helpful because the country of origin does not necessarily reveal the origin of component technology that a supplier integrates into the final product.

Third, officials from the Central Intelligence Agency and the Director of National Intelligence stated that tracking the country of origin for every IT component used in the agency's telecommunications networks would be prohibitively expensive and infeasible, based on the mechanisms that are currently readily available.

CONCLUSION

IT supply chain risk management is an emerging and complex area. The organizations, people, activities, information, and resources used to create and distribute commercial IT to federal agencies introduce a myriad of security risks to federal information systems. If exploited, supply chain vulnerabilities—such as purchasing IT from gray markets or poor inspection and testing procedures—can introduce threats to the confidentiality, integrity, and availability of federal information systems. Should this occur on a critical information system, the potential exists for serious adverse impact on an agency's operations, assets, or employees.

Despite acknowledging these risks, the Departments of Energy and Homeland Security have not developed clear policies that define what security measures, if any, should be implemented to protect against supply chain threats.

Further, the Departments of Energy, Justice, and Homeland Security have neither developed and documented procedures for implementing supply chain protection measures nor established monitoring capabilities that are necessary to verify compliance with, and the effectiveness of, these measures. Until comprehensive policies, procedures, and monitoring capabilities are developed, documented, and implemented, it is more likely that these national security-related agencies will rely on security measures that are inadequate, ineffective, or inefficient to manage emergent information technology supply chain risks. In contrast, Defense has made greater progress by defining supply chain protection measures and implementing procedures.

RECOMMENDATIONS FOR EXECUTIVE ACTION

To assist three national security-related agencies in better addressing IT supply chain-related security risks for their departmental information systems, we are making the following eight recommendations.

To assist the Department of Energy in protecting against IT supply chain threats, we recommend that the Secretary of Energy direct the appropriate agency officials to take the following three actions:

- develop and document departmental policy that defines which security measures should be employed to protect against supply chain threats;
- develop, document, and disseminate procedures to implement the supply chain protection security measures defined in departmental policy; and
- develop and implement a monitoring capability to verify compliance with, and assess the effectiveness of, supply chain protection measures.

To assist the Department of Homeland Security in protecting against IT supply chain threats, we recommend that the Secretary of Homeland Security direct the appropriate agency officials to take the following three actions:

- develop and document departmental policy that defines which security measures should be employed to protect against supply chain threats;
- develop, document, and disseminate procedures to implement the supply chain protection security measures defined in departmental policy; and
- develop and implement a monitoring capability to verify compliance with, and assess the effectiveness of, supply chain protection measures.

To assist the Department of Justice in protecting against IT supply chain threats, we recommend that the Attorney General direct the appropriate agency officials to take the following two actions:

- develop, document, and disseminate procedures to implement the supply chain protection security measures defined in departmental policy; and
- develop and implement a monitoring capability to verify compliance with, and assess the effectiveness of, supply chain protection measures.

AGENCY COMMENTS AND OUR EVALUATION

We provided a draft of this report to the Departments of Defense, Energy, Homeland Security, and Justice (including the FBI), the Office of the Director of National Intelligence, and the Department of Commerce's NIST for their review and comment.

Energy provided written comments on a draft of our report. In its comments, Energy stated that it concurred with the spirit of our recommendations. Energy also expressed concern that the recommendations are not fully aligned with the administration's initiatives and stated that it believes policies and standards to address IT supply chain risk management must be coordinated at the national level, not independently through individual agencies. We agree that national or federal policies and standards should be coordinated and promulgated at the national or federal level. We also believe, as intended by our recommendations, that federal departments are responsible for developing departmental policies and procedures that are consistent and aligned with federal guidance. Our recommendations to Energy are based on and consistent with federal guidance on supply chain risk management. Energy also stated that our report may significantly underestimate the deep complexities and interdependencies posed by the supply chain threat. Our report recognizes the unique characteristics related to understanding and mitigating the risks associated with the emerging IT supply chain threat. In particular, we identified potential threats to federal information systems that are beyond the failure or disruption in the production or distribution of critical IT products, including the introduction of hardware or software containing malicious logic at any point in a system's life cycle.

DHS also provided written comments on a draft of our report (see app. III), signed by DHS's Director of Departmental GAO-OIG Liaison Office. In its comments, DHS concurred with our recommendations and stated that the department's Chief Information Security Officer had begun coordinating with the appropriate program offices to develop departmental policy to define security measures to protect against supply chain threats, with an estimated completion date of October 31, 2012. DHS also indicated that the Chief Information Security Officer will (1) examine the best available risk management procedures and (2) explore viable options for verifying compliance with, and assessing the effectiveness of, IT supply chain protection measures, with estimated completion dates of June 30, 2013, and October 31, 2013, respectively. We also received technical comments via e-mail from DHS officials responsible for IT supply chain-related efforts that were incorporated, where appropriate.

In addition, Justice concurred with the recommendations via an e-mail from the Acting Assistant Director, Audit Liaison Group, Internal Review and Evaluation Office, Justice Management Division. We also received technical comments via e-mail from FBI's audit liaison that were incorporated, where appropriate.

We also received technical comments via e-mail from additional officials responsible for IT supply chain-related efforts at Defense, Commerce's NIST, and the Office of the Director of National Intelligence. These comments were incorporated, where appropriate.

Gregory C. Wilshusen
Director
Information Security Issues

APPENDIX I: OBJECTIVES, SCOPE, AND METHODOLOGY

Our objectives were to identify (1) the key risks associated with the supply chains used by federal agencies to procure information technology (IT) equipment, software, or services; (2) the extent to which selected national security-related agencies have addressed information technology supply chain risks; and (3) the extent to which national security-related federal agencies have determined that their telecommunication networks contain foreign-developed equipment, software, or services.

To identify the key risks, we collected, reviewed, and analyzed relevant supply chain-related practices, guidance, reports, policies, articles, press releases, and other materials from the Departments of Commerce, Defense, Homeland Security (DHS), and Justice. We also collected, reviewed, and analyzed articles from organizations, such as the Information Assurance Technology Analysis Center, the Software Assurance Forum for Excellence in

Code, and the Supply Chain Management Center at the University of Maryland's Robert H. Smith School of Business. Using these materials, we identified supply chain-related threats and vulnerabilities based on whether multiple source documents acknowledged the same or similar threats. On the basis of our analysis, we created common descriptions of the key threats and vulnerabilities related to the supply chain. We then validated our list of key threats by sharing them with, and soliciting feedback from, officials from the Office of the Director of National Intelligence, the Office of the National Counterintelligence Executive, the Defense Intelligence Agency, the Central Intelligence Agency, and the National Security Agency.

To identify the extent to which selected national security-related agencies have addressed IT supply chain risks, we analyzed agency policies and procedures related to information security and system acquisition at the Departments of Energy, Justice, Homeland Security, and Defense. We selected these national security-related departments because each is authorized to perform duties connected to national security, law enforcement, intelligence, or homeland defense. In particular, we evaluated whether an agency had, consistent with National Institute of Standards and Technology (NIST) Special Publication 800-53 controls SA-1 and SA-12, defined measures and developed implementing procedures to protect against information technology supply chain threats. We did not assess the effectiveness or legality of any defined measures or developed implementing procedures. In addition, we interviewed officials at each of the four agencies. For Energy, we interviewed officials from the National Nuclear Security Administration Office of the Chief Information Officer; Department of Energy Office of the Chief Information Officer; the Office of Health, Safety, and Security; the Office of Security Technology and Assistance; and the Office of Intelligence and Counterintelligence. For Justice, we interviewed officials from the Federal Bureau of Investigation and the Justice Management Division. For DHS, we interviewed officials from the National Cyber Security Division (Supply Chain Risk Management Group), the Office of the Chief Information Officer/Security Officer, and the Intelligence and Analysis Office. For Defense, we interviewed officials from the Defense Intelligence Agency, the Office of the Defense Chief Information Officer (Trusted Mission Systems and Networks), the Office of the Under Secretary of Defense for Acquisition, Technology, and Logistics (Systems Engineering), the National Security Agency, the Defense Information Assurance Program, and the U.S. Army.

To identify the extent to which national security-related federal agencies have determined that their telecommunications networks contain foreign-developed equipment, software, or services, we conducted a legal analysis and interviewed agency officials. Specifically, to determine whether agencies were required to make determinations related to the presence of foreign-developed equipment, software, or services in their telecommunications networks, we analyzed federal statutes, regulations, and agency policies. Sources consulted include provisions of the United States Code such as the Buy American Act, as well as other public laws; the Federal Acquisition Regulation and relevant supplements, including the Defense Federal Acquisition Regulation Supplement; Defense Federal Acquisition Regulation Procedures, Guidance, and Information; Department of Homeland Security procurement regulations; Office of Management and Budget Circular A-130; selected Homeland Security Presidential Directives; selected Executive Orders; and related GAO products. To determine whether the selected national security-related federal agencies had made determinations related to the presence of foreign-developed equipment, software, or services on their telecommunications networks, we interviewed officials from Justice's Management Division and the Offices of the Chief Information Officer for the Departments of Energy, Homeland Security, and Defense. In order to identify potential costs and benefits associated with tracking the country of origin of IT equipment, software or services, we also interviewed officials from the Director of National Intelligence, the Defense Intelligence Agency, the National Security Agency, and the Central Intelligence Agency.

We conducted this performance audit from November 2010 through March 2012 in accordance with generally accepted government auditing standards. Those standards require that we plan and perform the audit to obtain sufficient, appropriate evidence to provide a reasonable basis for our findings and conclusions based on our audit objectives. We believe that the evidence obtained provides a reasonable basis for our findings and conclusions based on our audit objectives.

End Notes

[1] The National Institute of Standards and Technology (NIST) has defined the term "supply chain" to mean a set of organizations, people, activities, information, and resources for creating and moving a product or service from suppliers through to an organization's customers. Also, NIST defines "information technology" as any equipment or interconnected system or subsystem of equipment that is used in the automatic acquisition, storage, manipulation, management, movement, control, display, switching, interchange, transmission, or reception

of data or information. This includes, among other things, computers, software, firmware, and services (including support services).

[2] Director of National Intelligence, *Worldwide Threat Assessment of the U.S. Intelligence Community,* unclassified statement for the record, Senate Select Committee on Intelligence (Washington, D.C.: Jan. 31, 2012).

[3] GAO's biennial high-risk list identifies government programs that have greater vulnerability to fraud, waste, abuse, and mismanagement or need transformation to address economy, efficiency, or effectiveness challenges. We have designated federal information security as a high-risk area since 1997; in 2003, we expanded this high-risk area to include protecting systems supporting our nation's critical infrastructure. See, most recently, GAO, *High-Risk Series: An Update*, GAO-11-278 (Washington, D.C.: February 2011).

[4] GAO first designated Department of Defense business systems modernization as high risk in 1995 and designated implementing and transforming the Department of Homeland Security as a high-risk area in 2003.

[5] According to NIST, risk is a measure of the extent to which an entity is threatened by a potential circumstance or event, and typically a function of (1) the adverse impacts that would arise if the circumstance or event occurs, and (2) the likelihood of occurrence, which is based on an analysis of the probability that a given threat is capable of exploiting a given vulnerability. NIST defines "threat" as any circumstance or event with the potential to adversely impact organizational operations and assets, individuals, other organizations, or the nation through an information system via unauthorized access, destruction, disclosure, modification of information, and/or denial or disruption of service. NIST also defines "vulnerability" as a weakness in an information system, system security procedures, internal controls, or implementation that could be exploited by a threat.

[6] Carnegie Mellon University, Software Engineering Institute, *Evaluating and Mitigating Software Supply Chain Security Risks*, CMU/SEI-2010-TN-016 (Pittsburgh, Pa.: May 2010).

[7] A supplier of information technology elements or services is also an acquirer of subelements that make up the products. Each subelement may have its own supply chain.

[8] Firmware is defined as the combination of a hardware device and computer instructions and data that reside as read-only software on that device.

[9] OMB, *Management of Federal Information Resources*, Circular A-130 (Washington, D.C.: November 28, 2000).

[10] GAO, *Cybersecurity: Progress Made but Challenges Remain in Defining and Coordinating the Comprehensive National Initiative*, GAO-10-338 (Washington, D.C.: Mar. 5, 2010).

[11] Title III of the E-Government Act of 2002, Pub. L. No. 107-347, Dec. 17, 2002.

[12] FISMA requires that federal agencies comply with NIST information security standards, and agencies may not waive their use. In addition, FISMA requires agencies to develop, document, and implement agencywide programs to provide security for the information systems that support their operations and assets.

[13] NIST, *Federal Information Processing Standards (FIPS) Publication 199: Standards for Security Categorization of Federal Information and Information Systems* (Gaithersburg, Md.: February 2004).

[14] NIST defines "high," "moderate," and "low impact" with respect to consequences of loss of confidentiality, integrity or availability. Thus, high, moderate, and low impact correspond, respectively; to catastrophic, serious, or limited adverse effect on organizational operations, organizational assets, or individuals.

[15] NIST, *FIPS Publication 200: Minimum Security Requirements for Federal Information and Information Systems* (Gaithersburg, Md.: March 2006).

[16] NIST, *Recommended Security Controls for Federal Information Systems and Organizations*, SP 800-53, Revision 3 (Gaithersburg, Md.: May 2010).

[17] SA-12 states that an organization should define and employ a list of measures to protect against supply chain threats as part of a comprehensive, defense-in-breadth information security strategy. According to SP 800-53, Revision 3, SA-12 should be selected for the initial control baseline of all agency information systems categorized as high impact.

[18] NIST defines "penetration testing" as security testing in which evaluators mimic real-world attacks in an attempt to identify ways to circumvent the security features of an application, system, or network.

[19] SA-1 states that organizations should develop formal, documented procedures to facilitate the implementation of system and services acquisition policy and associated system and services acquisition family of controls, which includes SA-12. According to SP 800-53, Revision 3, SA-1 should be selected for the initial control baseline regardless of categorization.

[20] The Committee on National Security Systems was established by National Security Directive 42 to, among other things, issue policy directives and instructions that provide mandatory information security requirements for national security systems. The committee is chaired by the Department of Defense.

[21] The Committee on National Security Systems Instruction 1253, *Security Categorization and Control Selection for National Security Systems*, October 2009.

[22] The impact level for a national security system is determined using the Committee on National Security Systems Instruction 1253 instead of FIPS 199. The instruction uses a more granular structure in which the potential impact levels of loss of confidentiality, integrity, and availability are individually used to select categorization.

[23] NIST, *Managing Information Security Risk: Organization, Mission, and Information System View*, SP 800-39 (Gaithersburg, Md.: March 2011).

[24] The act defines "supply chain risk" as "risk that an adversary may sabotage, maliciously introduce unwanted function, or otherwise subvert the design, integrity, manufacturing, production, distribution, installation, operation, or maintenance of a covered system so as to surveil, deny, disrupt, or otherwise degrade the function, use, or operation of such system."

[25] NIST, *Piloting Supply Chain Risk Management Practices for Federal Information Systems,* Draft NISTIR 7622 (Gaithersburg, Md.: June 2010).

[26] NIST, *Security and Privacy Controls for Federal Information Systems and Organizations*, Draft SP 800-53, Revision 4 (Gaithersburg, Md.: February 2012).

[27] Supply chain-related threat actors include corporate spies, corrupt government officials, cyber vandals, disgruntled employees, foreign military, government agents or spies, radical activists, purveyors of counterfeit goods, or criminals.

[28] GAO, *Cyber Analysis and Warning: DHS Faces Challenges in Establishing a Comprehensive National Capability*, GAO-08-588 (Washington, D.C.: July 31, 2008).

[29] Hewlett-Packard (HP) Company, HP Software Security Response Team, *HP Support Document: Support Communications–Security Bulletin, HP USB Floppy Drive Key (Option) for ProLiant Servers, Local Virus Infection*, April 3, 2008, http://bizsupport1.austin.hp.com/bizsupport/TechSupport/Document.jsp?objectID=c01404 119, accessed March 21, 2012; and Liam Tung, "HP Ships USB Sticks with Malware," *CNET News*, April 9, 2008. http://news.cnet.com/HP-ships-USB-sticks-withmalware/2100-7349_3-6236976.html, accessed January 3, 2012.

[30] The United States Computer Emergency Readiness Team (US-CERT) is the operational arm of the National Cyber Security Division at DHS and is tasked with protecting the nation's information infrastructure by coordinating defense against and response to cyber attacks.

31 A "backdoor" is a general term for a malicious program that can potentially give an intruder remote access to an infected computer. At a minimum, most backdoors allow an attacker to perform a certain set of actions on a system, such as transferring files or acquiring passwords.

[32] Information Assurance Technology Analysis Center, *Security Risk Management for the Off-the-Shelf (OTS) Information and Communications Technology (ICT) Supply Chain An Information Assurance Technology Analysis Center (IATAC) State-of-the-Art Report,* DO 380 (Herndon, Va.: August 2010).

[33] The United States Attorney's Office, Southern District of Texas. *Two Charged with Selling Counterfeit Computer Products*, January 4, 2008. www.cybercrime.gov/edmanCharge.pdf, accessed January 31, 2012. The defendants in this investigation pleaded guilty to selling counterfeit Cisco products to the Federal Bureau of Prisons.

[34] Jim Handy, "Significant Potential Problems in Semiconductors," *Objective Analysis* (March 11, 2011), http://www.objective-analysis.com/uploads/2011-03-11_Major_Earthquake_Hits_Japan.pdf, accessed January 4, 2012.

[35] Rare earth elements can be used in a variety of commercial information technology equipment, such as cell phones and computer hard drives. Further, these elements are also critical to the development of sophisticated military applications, such as guidance and control systems and advanced communications systems.

[36] GAO, *Information Security: IRS Needs to Enhance Internal Control over Financial Reporting and Taxpayer Data,* GAO-11-308 (Washington, D.C.: Mar. 15, 2011).

[37] GAO, *Information Security: Cyber Threats and Vulnerabilities Place Federal Systems at Risk,* GAO-09-661T (Washington, D.C.: May 5, 2009).

[38] Department of Justice, *Manhattan U.S. Attorney and FBI Assistant Director-In-Charge Announce Arrest of Computer Programmer For Stealing Proprietary Code From the Federal Reserve Bank of New York* (January 18, 2012), http://www.justice.gov/usao/nys/pressreleases/January12/zhangboarrestpr.pdf, accessed February 6, 2012.

[39] Stacey Simpson, ed., Software Assurance Forum for Excellence in Code (SAFECode), *Software Integrity Controls: An Assurance-Based Approach to Minimizing Risks in the Software Supply Chain* (June 14, 2010).

[40] DHS, Industrial Control Systems Alert 11-346-01, "Schneider Electric Quantum Ethernet Module Multiple Vulnerabilities," December 12, 2011, https://www.us-cert.gov/control_systems/pdf/ICS-ALERT-11-346-01.pdf, accessed February 6, 2012. Control systems are computer-based systems that monitor and control sensitive processes and physical functions and perform vital functions in many of our nation's critical infrastructures, including electric power, oil and gas, water treatment, and chemical production.

[41] A denial of service is a method of attack from a single source that denies system access to legitimate users by overwhelming the target computer with messages and blocking legitimate traffic. It can prevent a system from being able to exchange data with other systems or use the Internet.

[42] FISMA permits an agency to use more stringent information security standards if it certifies that its standards are at least as stringent as the NIST standards and are otherwise consistent with policies and guidelines issued under FISMA.

[43] Defense subsequently reissued the policy and extended it through March 2012. Directive-Type Memorandum 09-016, *Supply Chain Risk Management to Improve the Integrity of Components Used in DoD Systems* (March 10, 2010).

[44] Trusted Mission Systems and Networks is the Defense organization that is responsible for, among other things, leading the department's supply chain risk management pilot effort, providing required quarterly and final reports for CNCI Initiative 11, and developing and updating the supply chain risk management Pilot Program Key Practices and Implementation Guide and Concept of Operations.

[45] Defense released a previous version of the guide in 2009.

[46] Defense defines "critical program information" as elements or components of a research, development, and acquisition program that, if compromised, could cause significant degradation in mission effectiveness; shorten the expected combat-effective life of the system; reduce technological advantage; significantly alter program direction; or enable an adversary to defeat, counter, copy, or reverse engineer the technology or capability.

[47] A milestone decision can be defined as a point at which a recommendation is made and approval is sought regarding starting or continuing an acquisition program (i.e., proceeding to the next phase).

[48] Committee on National Security Systems, Directive 505, *Supply Chain Risk Management* (Mar. 7, 2012).

[49] Formerly an independent agency, the Office of the National Counterintelligence Executive is now a component of the Office of the Director of National Intelligence. The duties of the National Counterintelligence Executive are set forth in part in the Counterintelligence Enhancement Act of 2002. One of these duties is to act in coordination with other agencies to assess the vulnerabilities of the U.S. government, as well as the private sector, to intelligence threats in order to identify the areas, programs, and activities that require protection from such threats.

[50] The Berry Amendment could apply where the Secretary of Defense, upon the recommendation of the Strategic Materials Protection Board pursuant to 10 U.S.C. 187, determines that the domestic availability of a particular electronic component is critical to national security.

INDEX

M

N

O

P

Q

R

U

V

W